Cross Cultural Communication

· · · · · · · · · · · ·

*A Guide for
International
Students*

© 2009, 2010, 2014 Carrie C. Hutchinson
721 Cliff Drive
Santa Barbara, CA 93109
Phone 805.965.0581

Table of Contents

Diversity

"Diversity, generally understood and embraced, is not casual liberal tolerance of anything and everything not yourself. It is not polite accommodation. Instead, diversity is, in action, the sometimes painful awareness that other people, other races, other voices, other habits of mind, have as much integrity of being, as much claim upon the world, as you do. No one has an obligation greater than your own to change, or yield, or to assimilate into the mass.

The irreconcilable is as much a part of social life as the congenial. Being strong in life is being strong amid differences while accepting the fact that your own self can be a considerable imposition upon everyone you meet.

I urge you to consider your own oddity before you are troubled or offended by that of others. And I urge you, amid all the differences present to the eye and mind, to reach out and create the bonds that will sustain the commonwealth that will protect us all. We are meant to be here together."

William M. Chace
The Language of Action, 1989

Chapter 1

The U.S. College and Classroom

Learning Objectives

After studying this chapter, you should be able to:

1. Describe the levels of the U.S. higher education system.

2. Describe types of higher educational institutions in the U.S.

3. Explain the expectations for student behavior in the U.S. classroom.

4. Explain how your professors calculate your grade.

5. Explain what constitutes plagiarism, cheating, and sharing answers, and describe the repercussions of academic dishonesty.

Chapter Outline

- Introduction
- United States Higher Education
  - Degrees of Higher Education
  - Additional Higher Education Terms
  - How to Learn What Classes are Offered by a College or University
- Types of Higher Education Institutions in the U.S.
- U.S. Classroom Expectations
  - Communicating in Class
  - Communicating Outside of Class: Office Hours
- Grading Criteria for U.S. Colleges and Universities
  - Grade Point Average
- Academic Integrity
- Chapter Summary
- Key Terms

Introduction

This course is designed to help you transition from your home culture and academic system to the academic system of your host culture. In this section you will learn some basic terminology to help you understand your experience on your new college campus, including what is expected of you as a student in the classroom, and how you can achieve the grades you desire. This information is just a start. There is much more to learn, but much of it will be learned through experience. If you have questions about what is expected of you to succeed in your classes, the best way to find out is to ask your professors. For now, here is a basic guide to the U.S. higher education system.

United States Higher Education

Education is free and required of U.S. citizens from kindergarten (age 5) to 12th grade (age 18) – the last year of high school. It is free to all citizens. Students usually change schools after 6th grade (elementary school), and after 8th or 9th grade (junior high school). Students finish their education in high school, which goes up to grade 12. After high school students must pay for their education, and different schools have different costs depending on whether they are public or private, and whether they are two-year or four-year institutions.

"Higher education" is any schooling that takes place after the 12th grade. In the United States, a person may apply to enroll in higher education at any time in his or her life. Students who enroll in higher education after high school are commonly referred to as "traditional age" college students. Those who enroll later in life are often called "re-entry students" or "mature students."

Degrees of Higher Education

There are several levels in higher education. An **Associate's Degree** (A.A.) is a two-year degree. Students can stop their education after they have achieved an Associate's Degree, or they can transfer to a four-year institution to work toward a Bachelor's Degree, majoring in a specific field.

A **Bachelor's Degree (B.A.)** is a degree granted by a four-year institution. Students receive a Bachelor's Degree in their major and may also have their minor listed on their diploma.

A **Master's Degree (M.A.)** is an advanced degree granted by a graduate program, which usually takes one to three years to complete beyond a B.A degree. Some Universities offer graduate programs while some do not. Professors at a Community College must have at least a Mater's Degree in the field they are teaching.

A **Doctorate: (Ph.D.)** is an advanced degree granted by a graduate program at a University, which usually takes between five to seven years to complete after a B.A degree. Some graduate programs offer a Doctorate and some only offer a Master's Degree. A doctorate is the highest level of education that can be achieved in the U.S.

Additional Higher Education Terms

Here are a few additional terms you should know to help you understand your experience at a higher education institution in the U.S.:

Diploma: Certificate that demonstrates completion of a degree.

General Education: Students are required to take classes outside of their chosen field of study in order to have a more comprehensive overall education. These courses fulfill what is called a "G.E. requirement."

Major: A student's chosen field of study.

Minor: A student's chosen field in addition to their major. Getting a "minor" in a field requires fewer classes than a major.

Extracurricular Activities: American students in high school and college may be members of interest groups such as sports teams, musical ensembles, community service groups, business clubs, theater clubs, and many more. These are considered "extracurricular activities" and they are often considered helpful when trying to get accepted into a four-year university. A four-year college or university accepts students based on their grades, test scores, extracurricular activities, and usually a written essay. Not all students who apply to major universities are accepted (see the difference between a university and community college below).

Transfer: Many college students attend a small two-year college before they finish their education at a four-year university. When they move from one college to another college or university it is called "transferring." Many students will say "I plan to transfer to UCSB after I finish my general education."

How to Learn What Classes are Offered by a College or University

You can learn more about the institution you are attending or would like to attend by looking at the **Course Catalog**, which lists all courses offered by the school and is updated every few years.

You can see a list of specific classes offered each semester by looking at your school's **Schedule of Classes**, which is published in print and online before the start of each semester.

Activity

List how your country's education system is different than that in the United States:

_____
_____
_____
_____
_____

Types of Higher Education Institutions in the U.S.

There are several types of higher education institutions in the United States. This is a brief overview of each system so you can better understand the structure of the institution you are attending.

A **community college**, sometimes called a "Junior College," offers a two-year degree called an Associate's Degree, which is usually designed to prepare students to transfer to a four-year university to study their major. Community Colleges may also offer certificates in vocational training. Community Colleges do not offer a B.A., M.A., or Ph.D. Students do not compete to get into community colleges: anyone who fills out an application and pays the tuition is accepted.

A **college** is an institution that mostly offers a B.A., and has limited if any graduate courses and programs. Colleges can be public or private. Students compete to get accepted to a college, and although colleges accept large numbers of students, not all those who apply get accepted. Acceptance depends on grades, test scores, extracurricular activities, and usually a written essay.

A **university** offers a B.A. and usually also has graduate programs that offer an M.A. or Ph.D. Universities can be private or public. Students compete to get accepted to a university, and because universities are more competitive than colleges many students do not get accepted, especially at private universities. Acceptance depends on grades, test scores, extracurricular activities, and usually a written essay.

There are also various types of post-secondary schools and institutes that are mostly devoted to learning specific trades such as electronics, computers and cosmetology. Such schools do not usually award degrees, but instead prepare students for the working world.

Activity

List the different types of schools in the higher education system of your country:

_____
_____
_____
_____

U.S. Classroom Expectations

Each course has a course **syllabus** that the instructor will give to you the first week of classes. Here you will find all of the information that you will need to succeed in the course, including the location of the instructor's office and how to contact him or her, the goals of the course, the textbook and other materials, and a description of all assignments and when they are due.

Punctuality is a very important characteristic to demonstrate in an American classroom. It is expected that you will arrive to class before the official start time and be prepared to begin listening at the class's start time (which is listed in the schedule of classes). Many instructors will "take roll" by calling out students' names or passing around a sign-in sheet at the start of class. If you are not in class when the instructor takes roll you should expect to be considered absent from class that day. Missing class may affect your participation grade for the course, so make sure to check each instructor's policy listed on the syllabus.

Activity

What are the rules and expectations regarding punctuality in your culture?

_____
_____
_____
_____

Communicating in Class

Instructors in the U.S. vary on how they prefer to communicate with students. Some professors prefer to be called by their title (Professor Smith, Dr. Smith), while others prefer to be called by their first name. Usually a professor will tell students what to call him or her, or you can ask if you are not sure. A Harvard University study on successful college students found that successful students took the time to get to know their professors by talking to them before or after class and during office hours. Keep in mind that when you communicate with your professors you are making an impression. Even if you are communicating over email, make sure your communication is courteous and professional, and does not contain grammar or spelling errors.

U.S. classrooms are much more "interactive" than many other classrooms around the world. When instructors see a student remaining quiet in class, they might think that student is not interested or does not understand the course content. When instructors ask a question they expect students to respond. When a question is asked, you can raise your hand to show that you would like to respond. Students are also expected to raise their hands and ask questions about any information that is unclear. If you need help understanding a concept, raise your hand in class and ask for clarification. For example, you might say, "Professor Jones, I don't understand the meaning of metamorphosis. Could you explain it again?"

Students are expected to interact with their classmates during activities. The instructor will tell you when you are expected to discuss an idea with classmates in small groups. However, it is not expected that you will talk to classmates while the instructor is teaching a lesson. Although professors want an interactive class, if the professor or another student is commenting, other student "side conversations" in the class will be distracting and your professor will ask you to stop chatting.

Activity

What are the rules and expectations from your culture regarding communicating in class? How do you plan to overcome any differences in the expectations between your own culture and the U.S. culture?

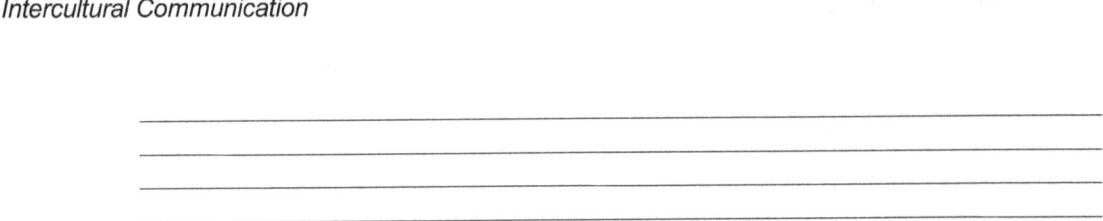

Communicating Outside of Class:

Office Hours

Instructors are required to be in their office to meet with students at consistent times each week. A professor will list his or her office hours on the syllabus for the course. If you are not comfortable raising your hand in class, you should visit your instructor during office hours. Students should not come to the instructor's office outside of the designated office hours and expect to be helped because instructors are usually grading papers or preparing for class. If you are not available during your instructor's office hours you should ask if you can make an appointment to see him or her.

Grading Criteria for U.S. Colleges and Universities

Instructors will evaluate your work in a class based on the following criteria, and these grades will result in a final grade for the course:

If you receive 90%-100% of the points available, this is an A. "A" work requires student performance above and beyond the average student. "A" work is truly exemplary, demonstrating a thorough understanding of course material and appropriate application of relevant concepts. Do not expect to receive an A unless the quality of your work is superior to the majority of the students in the class.

If you receive 80%-89% of the points available, this is a B. "B" work is above average, with the student completing all assignments in a competent fashion. "B" work is characterized by a good understanding of course material and a demonstrated ability to apply those concepts.

If you receive 70%-79% of the points available, this is a C. "C" work is average and simply meets the minimum requirements of the course. "C" work demonstrates a basic understanding of course material and a fair ability to apply course concepts.

If you receive 60-69% of the points available, this is a D. "D" work is below average and does not fully meet the minimum requirements of the course. "D" work is characterized by an incomplete understanding of course material and limited ability to apply course concepts.

If you receive 0-59% of the points available, this is an F. "F" work does not meet the minimum requirements of the course in any way. "F" work is characterized by a lack of understanding of course material and inability to apply course concepts.

Sometimes students request an incomplete grade for a course. "I" (Incompletes) will only be considered if the student has completed 75% of the course with a passing grade (C) and encounters some unforeseen circumstances that prevent her/him from completing the class (e.g., medical emergency, called to active military duty). The student must provide sufficient documentation concerning the circumstances.

In the U.S. each instructor will tell you how many points are available in the course and how many points you need to achieve to obtain each grade at the end of the course (an A, B, C, D, or F).

Please be aware that the grading criteria in the U.S are objective, which means that you cannot negotiate for a different grade. You will receive your course grade depending on how many points you accumulate throughout the semester. Please do not try to talk your professor into giving you a different grade at the end of the semester than the one designated by the points you have earned: this is considered unethical and the professor will not change your grade. If you have any questions about the points you receive on each assignment you need to ask the professor immediately after he or she has returned your assignment. Instructors will not change assignment grades at the end of the semester.

For example, if a course has 10 assignments, each worth 100 points, there are 1000 points available in the course. Therefore:

If you achieved 90% or higher of 1000 (900-1000 points), you would receive an A.

If you achieved between 80% and 89% (800-895 points) you would receive a B.

If you achieved between 70% and 79% (700-795 points) you would receive a C.

If you achieved between 60% and 69% (600-695 points) you would receive a D.

If you achieved less than 60% (599 points or less) you would receive an F.

Grade Point Average

Your grade point average is an average of all your grades for all your college or university courses. Grade point average is commonly referred to by its initials, GPA. Students will ask each other, "What's your GPA?" They are referring to a system of points for courses taken.

A=4, B=3, C=2, D=1, F=0.

For example, if you took 5 courses in a semester for 15 units:

English 3 units X A (4) = 12
History 3 units X B (3) = 9
Math 3 units X C (2) = 6
Physics 3 units X D (1) = 3
Psychology 3 units X F (0) = 0
Total 15 units at 30 (12+9+6+3+0) make an average of 2.0 or C. This is the minimum average you need to stay in good standing academically.
In the case of a D or F, many students would choose to repeat the course.

Some students choose to take a class "Pass/No Pass." This means that you do not get a grade from your professor, but instead they report a P (Pass) or NP (No Pass) as your grade. Students choose to take a course Pass/No Pass if they are worried that their letter grade in the class will negatively affect their GPA. If you achieve a C or higher the grade shows on your transcript as a "Pass" (P), but if you get a D or lower it will be a "No Pass" (NP). Although Pass/No Pass courses will show on your transcript, **another institution may not accept the course because there is no letter grade reported.** If you decide to take a course Pass/No Pass make sure you understand the consequences and select this option by the deadline listed in the course schedule.

Activity

What is the grading system like in your culture? How do students receive grades and what do they mean?

_____

_____

_____

_____

_____

_____

_____

_____

Academic Integrity

All the work you complete for any class in the U.S. must be your own independent work and may not be partially or completely worked on by someone else, unless it is a group project and your instructor says it is a group project. **Academic misconduct** includes activities such as plagiarism, copying work from other students or sharing answers to exams or work that is expected to be completed by students individually. Each of the following constitutes academic misconduct, and will result in an F for the course you are taking, and possibly expulsion from the school:

Plagiarism includes stating information or ideas that were created by someone else and claiming they are your own ideas. **Copying** includes duplicating another student's work on an assignment that is supposed to be completed by students individually. All class assignments are supposed to be completed individually unless the instructor specifies that it is a group or team project. **Sharing Answers** involves working together on answers for assignments that are supposed to be completed by students individually, or giving another student your answers when they are supposed to find their own answers. For courses in the U.S., any of the above behaviors will result in a failing grade ("F") in the course. These rules are outlined in the standards for conduct on your school's webpage.

Activity

What are the rules and expectations regarding plagiarism and cheating in your culture? How is it different from the U.S.?

_____

_____

_____

_____

_____

_____

_____

_____

Chapter Summary

This chapter introduced you to the higher education system in the U.S. Levels of higher education were explained, including the degrees that are available. Expectations for classroom behavior were described, including behavior during class and outside of class with professors. You learned how grades are calculated by professors, and how you can keep track of your own grade point average. Finally, cheating, plagiarism, and sharing answers were defined to make sure that you do not commit academic dishonesty.

Key Terms

academic misconduct: activities such as plagiarism, copying work from other students or sharing answers to exams or work that is expected to be completed by students individually.

associate's degree (A.A.): a two-year degree.

bachelor's degree (B.A.): a degree granted by a four-year institution.

college: an institution that usually only offers a B.A., and has limited if any graduate courses and programs. Colleges can be public or private.

community college: an institution that offers a two-year degree called an associate's degree, which is usually designed to prepare students to transfer to a four-year university to study their major. Community colleges may also offer certificates in vocational training.

copying: behavior that includes duplicating another student's work on an assignment that is supposed to be completed by students individually.

course catalog: a large document that lists all courses offered by the school and is updated every few years.

diploma: certificate that demonstrates completion of a degree.

doctorate (Ph.D.): an advanced degree granted by a graduate program at a university, which usually takes between five to seven years to complete after a B.A degree.

extracurricular activities: interest groups such as sports teams, musical ensembles, community service groups, business clubs, or theater clubs.

general education: classes outside of a student's chosen field of study that allow for a more comprehensive overall education.

grade point average (GPA): an average of all your grades for all your college or university courses.

major: a student's chosen field of study.

master's degree (M.A.): an advanced degree granted by a graduate program, which usually takes one to three years to complete beyond a B.A degree.

minor: a student's chosen field in addition to their major.

office hours: the hours during which instructors are required to be in their office to meet with students at consistent times each week. A professor will list his or her office hours on the syllabus for the course.

plagiarism: behavior that includes stating information or ideas that were created by someone else and claiming they are your own ideas.

schedule of classes: a document that lists specific classes offered each semester.

sharing answers: behavior that includes working together on answers for assignments that are supposed to be completed by students individually, or giving another student your answers when they are supposed to find their own answers.

syllabus: a document provided by your instructor that contains all of the information that you will need to succeed in the course, including the location of the instructor's office and how to contact him or her, the goals of the course, the textbook and other materials, and a description of all assignments and when they are due.

transfer: when a student moves from one college to another college or university.

university: an institution that offers a B.A. and usually also have graduate programs that offer an M.A. or Ph.D. Universities can be private or public.

CHAPTER 1 ACTIVITIES

Journal

Use this page to respond to the question assigned by your instructor upon completion of this chapter.

Plagiarism & Academic Dishonesty

Case studies provided by Carola Smith, Director of International Education, Santa Barbara City College

1. The instructor gives students a list of study questions before the final exam and tells students that it is ok to study for the exam in groups. A number of students in the class decide to each prepare the answer to one question and to share their prepared answers with the other students in their study group. In preparation for the exam, the students memorize the answers to the study questions. On the day of the exam, several students write down exactly the same answers to the exam questions. When the instructor realizes that the students' answers are identical, all students in the study group are given an "F" in the exam. How would this incident be handled by an instructor in your home country?

2. A student allows another student to copy his homework assignment before class. Would it be acceptable in your home country to copy each other's home work assignments?

3. A student who has just finished taking a test provides another student who has to take the test at a later time with the exam questions. Is it ok to share exam questions if you don't share the answers to the questions?

4. In preparation for an exam, a non-native speaker of English enters the definitions of terms, which are going to be tested on her biology exam, into her digital translating device. During the exam, she looks up the definitions. Is this acceptable, since the student does not speak English as fluently as her American classmates?

5. A student enters the answers to some of the more complex study questions for an exam into her cell phone. The answers, which are saved on the cell phone, are her original work. During the exam, the student refers to the some of the answers to make sure that she did not forget any important points. Is this considered cheating?

6. A student asks another student in the class to help him with a take-home exam. His friend provides him with most of the answers to the take-home exam questions. The student writes down the answers provided by his friend, and turns in the exam as his own work. Is it ok to help each other with take-home exams, which are supposed to be completed individually?

7. Each day at the beginning of class, the instructor passes around a sign-in sheet. A student, whose friend has missed class several times this semester and who is absent again, decides to sign in for her friend to avoid her from getting dropped from the class. Is it ok to help out a friend or would this be considered cheating?

8. A student has to write a paper on a well-known author. He decides to browse the Internet and finds several articles on this particular author. He uses a couple of sentences directly from the Internet and closely paraphrases several other sentences from the web articles without using quotation marks and without acknowledging the source. How do you think your instructors in the U.S. would handle a case like this?

9. A student has written a research paper for her global studies class, for which she received an A. In the following semester, she takes a class in intercultural communication. One of the course assignments is to write a research paper on a topic of choice. The student submits the same research paper, which she wrote for her other class. Could this be considered plagiarism?

Plagiarism Quiz

Put a check by the items that are considered plagiarism.

_____ 1. You like what an author says in a book, so you use her ideas in your own paper for a class, and you do not list her as the inventor of the idea.

_____ 2. You have a friend who already wrote a paper on a topic you have to write on so you borrow it and use some of his ideas without citing that the ideas belong to him.

_____3. You find research in the library and use it to support your ideas, citing each source of information.

_____4. You use the words of an expert to define a concept in your paper, and you do not list the source of the definition.

___5. You get a good idea for a speech from one you saw on the Internet, so you give the same speech in your Public Speaking class.

Put a check by the items that are considered cheating.

___1. You work with a friend on a paper for one of your classes but you each turn in your own paper with only your own name on it.

___2. You create one study guide with a friend and you both use it to study for an exam.

___3. You submit someone else's old paper but put your own name on it.

___4. You give one of your old papers to a friend, knowing that he plans to turn it in with his own name on it.

___5. Someone gives you a copy of a test from the class you are taking and you use it to study for the exam you are about to take.

Chapter 2

Intercultural Communication Competence

Learning Objectives

After studying this chapter, you should be able to:

1. Define intercultural communication.

2. Understand the requirements for communication competence.

3. Explain the stages of intercultural communication competence and assess which stage you are currently in.

4. Identify the stages of culture shock and re-entry shock.

5. Develop realistic expectations for what you will gain from learning about this subject.

Chapter Outline

- Introduction
- Intergroup and Intercultural Communication
- How Can You Improve Your Own Intercultural Communication?
    - How Does One Achieve Intercultural Communication Competence?
    - A Model of the Process of Communication Competence
- Culture Shock: Intercultural Communication on the Road
    - Re-Entry Shock
- Creating Realistic Goals
- Chapter Summary
- Key Terms

Introduction

Today it is easier than ever to visit a foreign country. You can see the Amazon jungle by turning on the television, you can be transported to India by watching a blockbuster movie, and, if you have the resources, you can jump on a plane and go almost anywhere your heart desires. Furthermore, you can engage in regular interactions with people halfway around the world just by getting online or picking up the phone. In 2005, Thomas Freidman published a book called *The World is Flat*, in which he claims that every corner of our world is becoming more and more accessible due to new technologies that allow us to communicate with people across the world as if they were right next door. Right now gamers in Tokyo are online with kids in Chicago that they have never personally met, playing a game and interacting as if they were in the same room; at this moment a woman in Bangalore is taking a pizza order placed by a Californian who will receive the pizza at his doorstep within 25 minutes; and everyday regular people get on planes to travel across the world for a quick meeting and then turn right back around and come home. As the world becomes even "flatter" our interactions with people from other cultures are on the rise. Ten years from now most people will not be able to go a single day without interacting with someone from another culture. Therefore, it is becoming more important than ever to become not only culturally aware, but also inter-culturally competent.

Consider the following scenario:

> *Maya is a sales manager at a large company in New York City. Her sales team has been invited to Saudi Arabia to pitch a new product to a very conservative, family-run organization. The new business partnership will potentially generate a great deal of revenue for her company. Once her team arrives and has several meetings with the potential buyers, she encounters a problem: at the end of the last meeting she is asked to leave the room so that the final decisions can be made and she suspects that she is being asked to do so because she is a woman. This request is disconcerting, considering that she is not only the manager of the team, but the highest paid and most experienced employee of her company. Maya is taken aback by this request and has no idea how to respond. She doesn't want to insult her hosts (especially*

because there is a lot of money to be made by the deal), but she is highly offended by their request.

This scenario highlights several issues that arise in intercultural interactions. First, Maya runs the risk of being *offensive* or inconsiderate to her hosts, depending on her response. This problem demonstrates the ethical challenges that accompany many intercultural interactions. She wants to behave according to her own ethical code, but she is starting to see that what is considered "good behavior" may be culturally relative. Second, Maya is concerned about losing the deal, so another goal is to be *effective*. This chapter will address the many challenges of being both effective and considerate when communicating with people in our diverse world. We'll begin by explaining what is meant by intercultural communication, and help you understand what it means to have intercultural competence. By the time you finish this chapter you should be able to set some realistic goals for yourself as you navigate our flattening world.

Intergroup and Intercultural Communication

Intergroup communication is defined as communication between people from two different groups. A group can be anything from a gender group to a cultural group, or even a sports team. If the definition of a group is so wide-ranging, you can imagine that each person has multiple group memberships at any given time. When you are communicating with someone you are usually aware of his or her gender, age, and culture, and maybe even some other groups to which he or she belongs. These details may or may not be important, but the moment any of these group memberships become important, you are engaging in an **intergroup interaction**. Thus, *theories* of intergroup communication strive to *explain* the behavior that goes on between people any time those individuals are aware of how their group memberships are the same as or different from one another.

For example, imagine that Emma, a female international student from Sweden, is talking to a fellow Swedish student named Frederick and another female classmate named Gina (who is American). Frederick makes a comment about how girls are obsessed with fashion. Because Emma is a woman this offensive comment makes her feel separate from Frederick and closer to Gina in such a way that he suddenly becomes an **outgroup member** and Gina becomes an **ingroup member**. However, the first important thing to understand about intergroup communication is that your own identity shifts and changes depending on the person you are talking to and what is being said. In the same scenario above, imagine that Frederick instead makes a comment saying, "American girls are obsessed with fashion." Now Emma shares a group membership with Frederick; he is suddenly an ingroup member and Gina is an outgroup member.

The second important thing to understand about intergroup communication is that whether you perceive someone as an ingroup member or outgroup member at any given moment affects the way you react to that person, both verbally and nonverbally. Being aware of the effects created by intergroup situations will allow you to be a much better communicator in all contexts.

An important context we'll focus on in this text is the intercultural context. **Intercultural communication** occurs when *culture* is the group membership that makes the communicators different from one another. Since the primary context of study for this course is the intercultural context, we need to decide what we mean by "culture" before we proceed. There are three common ways we refer to someone's background. **Race** is based on the genetically transmitted physical characteristics of a group of people who are classified together. **Ethnicity** is a social classification based on a variety of factors that are shared by a group of people who also share a common geographic origin or location. However, here our focus is on **culture**, which is a *learned* system of knowledge, behaviors, attitudes, beliefs, values, and norms that are shared by a group of people. You are not born with culture: you learn it through your interactions with others who show you the norms and rules of the society in which you live. **Norms** are ideas held by most members of the society about what is appropriate and expected behavior. The key to understanding your own and other cultures is knowing that there is no such thing as "normal" behavior. You only know what is normal because you have been taught the norms of your culture from the moment you were born by observing other members of your group.

We often learn culture through **enculturation**, which is the process of communicating a group's culture from one generation to the next. Often the transmission of one culture to another can be seen through **cultural elements**, or things that represent aspects of a culture such as music, art, food, and social institutions such as schools or governments. For example, an Asian American raised by her Chinese grandmother may consider herself an American girl, although she has learned to cook Chinese food from her grandmother and her house contains various artifacts from China. Furthermore, in her communication with others she may consciously or subconsciously use patterns of communication typical of her grandmother's culture.

Cultural elements are also transmitted through **acculturation**, which is the process through which an individual acquires new approaches, beliefs and values by coming into contact with other cultures to which they otherwise have no relation. Texans have become known for their Tex-Mex food, which was only possible through contact with their neighbors in Mexico. Communicatively, each group adopts words from the other culture, and this language adoption can result in shared values. Many Mexican-Americans speak *'Spanglish,'* adding English words into their Spanish dialect to describe things that have no direct translation in their native tongue. This natural occurrence stems from the need to integrate into one's social environment. Because it is so common for different cultures to come into contact, many people feel like they possess more than one culture. A **co-culture** is a distinct cultural group within a larger culture. For example, Mexican Americans are Americans who have a Mexican co-culture.

One main reason that our intercultural interactions can be confusing and frustrating is that our cultural differences are deeper than the cultural artifacts we see on the surface. For example, when you are visiting a foreign country and you strike up a conversation with a local person, it's obvious that you may be wearing different types of clothing and that you two may like different music, food, and activities. In addition to these differences, though, you also hold entirely different sets of beliefs and values, and this can make it difficult to really *understand* each other.

Intercultural experts often use the analogy of an iceberg to demonstrate the depths and complexities of culture. The cultural artifacts that you see are merely the "tip of the iceberg;" there are facets of culture that lie far beneath the surface and are not easily revealed unless you spend the time it takes to delve deeply into understanding that culture.

How Can You Improve Your Own Intercultural Communication?

Now that you've learned a little about the complexities of culture, you may be wondering how you can better understand the cultures you visit and successfully interact with people who have a culture different from yours. The next section is dedicated to understanding the process of learning communication competence and creating realistic goals for your experience.

How Does One Achieve Communication Competence?

In order to evaluate your own behavior in any intergroup interaction (whether it's between you and someone who is a different gender, age, or culture) you should know the criteria for evaluation. There are several indicators of competent communication, including that it is effective, appropriate, and adaptable.

Competent intergroup communication is effective. Competent communicators can realize their goals by communicating them well to others, even if those others are different. For this to happen your message must be understood, meaning that it should be clear, not ambiguous. Furthermore, to be effective means that your message must achieve its intended effect. A receiver not only has to understand what you need and want, but also has to agree to participate in its fruition. Goals are not always selfish; your goals can include the development or improvement of a relationship, the desire to help an important cause, to empathize with others, or to be a good employee. No matter what your goals are, your communication competence can be measured, in part, by your effectiveness in meeting the outcomes you desire even when the person on the receiving end is from another group. In the scenario described at the outset of this chapter, the American businesswoman, Maya, would have to find a way to communicate her need to be included in decision-making while still winning the business of her Saudi Arabian clients in order to be considered effective.

Competent intergroup communication is appropriate. To be appropriate, your message should consider time, place, and the overall context in which your communication is occurring. Clearly your *effectiveness* and *appropriateness* are inextricably linked: you will not be effective if you are inappropriate. This includes sensitivity to the feelings and attitudes of the listener. Sometimes we tend to be **egocentric communicators**, meaning that we are so wrapped up in our goals and needs that we create messages without giving much thought to the person who is listening. We also have a tendency to be **ethnocentric**, meaning we view and evaluate everyone's behavior through the lens of what is right and wrong in *our* culture. **Other-oriented communication** suggests that you consider the needs, expectations and wishes of the other person when sending a message. Occasionally this will include deciding to wait, and delivering a message at a better place and time. Thinking back again to our example, in order to be appropriate Maya may consider speaking in private to the manager of her client group so as not to cause an embarrassing scene.

Competent intergroup communication should demonstrate adaptability. Adaptability requires that you change what is not working. Often times we blame the receiver when our messages are misunderstood, but often it's ourselves who need to take a different approach. Adaptability includes the ability to try new things, which can be scary. Maya may want to consider sharing her opinions and final decisions with a male colleague and letting him deliver the message to her clients since it appears that they will not accept decisions coming from her. Although this approach may feel strange and not at all the way it would be done at home, it may be the right way to approach this situation if the goal is to be effective, appropriate, and adaptable.

Activity

When it comes to communicating with people in another culture, decide which part of competence has been your biggest challenge: being effective, being appropriate, or demonstrating adaptability? Why?

_____

_____

_____

_____

_____

How do you plan to overcome this challenge?

_____

_____

_____

_____

_____

_____

_____

_____

A Model of the Process of Communication Competence

Experts in communication competence suggest that there are three main pieces to achieving competence, which are knowledge, motivation, and skills. The **knowledge component** is the information you need to know about how people from your culture and other cultures communicate, and what it means to communicate effectively. From reading the last section you "know" what it takes to be a good communicator. This does not mean you necessarily want to be an effective communicator, or have the necessary skills. Thus, the second piece is the **motivational component**, which is the *desire* to be effective in your communication. However, just because you have the desire and the knowledge, does not mean you *know how* to do it. The **skills component** is the ability to apply a set of behaviors, often learned, that you can use to communicate well. Like with any skill, communication skills take practice; they do not always come naturally. Assuming you have the motivation to communicate effectively in intergroup settings such as those that involve intercultural communication, this text will give you the knowledge you'll need to *understand* the nature of intergroup communication, and provide you with some *skills* that will help you have more successful interactions.

The different pieces in the model of communication competence combine to form four levels of competence. The first stage is called **unconscious incompetence**, which is when you are not aware of the deficits in your skill set. This may describe your level of competence before taking this class. Imagine when you were a child and you were a passenger in your parent's car. You did not know how to drive, but driving was not required of you, so you did not think about it much; you had unconscious incompetence.

The second stage, **conscious incompetence,** is when you are aware of the areas in which you lack skills, but are not sure how to improve. Some people taking this course are in this stage. Imagine when you were about to get a driver's learning permit. You knew you did not know how to drive, but were ready to learn; you were consciously incompetent.

Stage three is termed **conscious competence**, which occurs when you are aware of how to improve your communication and you actively employ new strategies you've learned. During this stage it will likely feel awkward to use your new skills. Following the driving example, when you were learning to drive with a permit you had to actively apply your skills with great thought and attention. Do you remember the first time you drove on the highway? You had to pay close attention just to stay in the proper lane; your conscious competence now seems laughable!

Finally, the last stage is **unconscious competence**, when you are so accustomed to using your learned skills that they come naturally. This stage is where you will be long after this course is over and you continue to use the skills in your everyday life. It may take years to achieve this stage, and many people never achieve it. This is when you drive to work without even thinking about it. Sometimes you pull into the parking lot and realize you haven't been paying any attention to how you got there, but somehow your unconscious competence managed to help you arrive effectively (and safely)!

Activity

Describe your level of intercultural communication competence. Decide which stage you are at right now (unconscious incompetence, conscious incompetence, conscious competence, or unconscious competence) and explain why.

_____
_____
_____
_____
_____
_____
_____
_____
_____
_____
_____

Culture Shock: Intercultural Communication on the Road

If you happen to be taking this course before or during a trip abroad, one common phenomenon that you should expect to experience as you work your way through the steps toward cultural competence is **culture shock**. Culture shock comes from trying to navigate a new cultural environment and usually includes feelings of frustration, confusion, and even anger, stemming from a loss of the cultural cues and social norms to which you are accustomed. Culture shock manifests in several ways, and typically occurs in the following phases:

1. **The honeymoon phase:** This stage is signified by feelings of euphoria and excitement. The outsider may tend to notice things about the host culture that he or she prefers to his or her culture of origin.

   Typical thoughts in the honeymoon phase: "I love everything about this country. Every single person I meet is friendly and wonderful. People at home just aren't like this."

2. **The crisis/hostility phase:** This stage includes feelings of anxiety and even anger when faced with the norms of the host culture. The outsider may make comparisons between the host culture and culture of origin, in which the culture of origin always comes out in favor.

   Typical thoughts in the crisis/hostility phase: "What's with the bowing? Do they really need to bow every single time they greet each other? It seems so formal, it really makes me uncomfortable. I'm not doing it."

3. **The adjustment/humor phase:** This stage is characterized by the gradual acceptance that in order to function successfully in the host culture, the outsider must adjust his or her behavior and attitude. Over time the host culture's ways become more acceptable.

   Typical thoughts in the adjustment phase: "I have to remember to bow lower than Mr. Osaka since he's the President of the company. I hope I don't screw it up!"

4. **The adaptation phase:** This stage involves adopting a bi-cultural identity, whereby the outsider no longer considers him or herself a visitor, but rather integrates components of the host culture into his or her self-concept. This stage cannot be reached unless the outsider passes through the other stages, and desires integration.

   Typical thoughts in the adaptation phase: "I remember when I had to think so hard about how to greet a superior! Now I seem to do it

33

without thinking, and it's so nice to have such an easy way to show respect right off the bat."

The stages of culture shock often repeat until one becomes integrated into the new culture. Most visitors never get beyond the adjustment phase, and some even leave the host culture in the crisis phase. If you listen to people recount their travel stories you can usually identify which phase they were experiencing by how they describe their perception of the events that occurred.

Activity

Describe your experience so far with each of the stages of culture shock

1. The honeymoon phase: This stage is signified by feelings of euphoria and excitement. The outsider may tend to notice things about the host culture that he or she prefers to his or her culture of origin.

_____

_____

_____

_____

_____

2. The crisis/hostility phase: The outsider may make comparisons between the host culture and culture of origin, in which the culture of origin always comes out in favor. Frustration or anger is typical.

_____

_____

_____

_____

_____

3. The adjustment/humor phase: This stage is characterized by the gradual acceptance that in order to function successfully in the host culture, the outsider must adjust his or her behavior and attitude.

_____

_____

_____
_____
_____
_____

4. The adaptation phase: The outsider no longer considers him or herself a visitor, but rather integrates components of the host culture into his or her self-concept.

_____
_____
_____
_____
_____
_____

Re-Entry Shock

Culture shock does not end once you leave your host country and return home. After returning home to a place that was once familiar, you may find that you see things differently, almost as if you are a visitor in your own home country. You may see things through the eyes of the culture where you've been traveling, or you may just see things through the eyes of the new and more experienced person you've become. Either way, things will seem different to you, and this will cause **re-entry shock**. People suffering from re-entry shock often report:

→ Noticing details about their culture they did not notice before, which are often a *confirmation of the stereotypes* other cultures have about them

→ *Annoyance* with other people (even friends and family) who now seem ignorant about the world in general

→ A *feeling of superiority* and self-righteousness

→ *Surprise* at how disinterested others are in hearing about the trip

→ An *inability to describe* the complexities of the experience in a satisfying way

→ Depression and *loneliness*

When you return home after traveling, you have to pay special attention to avoid the same behaviors you attempted to avoid while traveling. Consider whether you are being egocentric when judging others' comments about your experience. Ask yourself why you are seeing things in a new light, and consider it a good thing. And most importantly, don't ever assume you are immune to culture shock just because you experienced it once or twice: culture shock will follow you to whichever far away land you visit in the future, no matter how much experience you have.

Creating Realistic Goals

Part of intergroup communication competence is having realistic expectations and goals, whether you are studying abroad or learning about group differences in your own country. Learning about communication can help you in certain ways and not in others. As stated above, *you should not expect to obtain unconscious competence during the span of this course.* Instead, consider this class an experiment where you are learning new strategies and testing them to determine whether you would like to keep them.

Something else to keep in mind as you proceed in this course is that you should not expect to be responsible for more than your share of the interaction. *The most you can do in any communication situation is 100% of your 50%.* Nothing more. You cannot do someone else's work for him or her, and each person has to be responsible for his or her half of the relationship. If another person is completely unwilling to do his or her share of work, there is nothing you can do except decide whether to continue trying or to give up. Once you have learned how to adapt to various types of people from different cultures and groups, you may become frustrated at how *inadaptable* most people tend to be! Try not to get frustrated with others, keeping in mind that you can only do *your* best.

One final thing to remember is that *learning about communication will not solve all problems.* Not all problems in the world are communication problems. Hopefully the information you learn here will give you a choice about what kind of communicator you want to be, and give you the tools you need to create the kinds of interactions you desire with people from other groups.

Chapter Summary

Learning about intergroup and intercultural communication can be a daunting process if you don't know what to expect. This chapter outlined what is meant by the study of intergroup and intercultural communication. The concept of communication competence was explained, so that you can assess where you are in the four-phase process of becoming a competent communicator. Next the stages of culture shock were described and some examples were given to help you identify your own stages. The chapter concluded with guidelines for establishing realistic expectations for what you will get out of a course in intergroup communication.

Key Terms

acculturation: the process through which an individual acquires new approaches, beliefs and values by coming into contact with other cultures to which they otherwise have no relation

adaptation phase: the stage of culture shock that involves adopting a bi-cultural identity, whereby the outsider no longer considers him or herself a visitor, but rather integrates components of the host culture into his or her self-concept

adjustment/humor phase: the stage of culture shock characterized by the gradual acceptance that in order to function successfully in the host culture, the outsider must adjust his or her behavior and attitude

co-culture: a distinct cultural group within a larger culture

conscious competence: when you are aware of how to improve and you can use new skills with effort.

conscious incompetence: when you are aware about the areas in which you lack skills, but are not sure how to improve

crisis/hostility phase: the stage of culture shock that includes feelings of anxiety and even anger when faced with the norms of the host culture

culture: a *learned* system of knowledge, behaviors, attitudes, beliefs, values, and norms that are shared by a group of people

cultural elements: things that represent aspects of a culture such as music, art, food, and social institutions such as schools or governments

culture shock: feelings that come from trying to navigate a new cultural environment that usually include frustration, confusion, and even anger, stemming from a loss of the cultural cues and social norms to which you are accustomed

egocentric communicators: communicators who are so wrapped up in their goals and needs that they create messages without giving much thought to the person who is listening

enculturation: the process of communicating a group's culture from one generation to the next

ethnicity: a social classification based on a variety of factors that are shared by a group of people who also share a common geographic origin or location

ethnocentric: the state of viewing and evaluating everyone's behavior through the lens of what is right and wrong in *one's own* culture

honeymoon phase: the stage of culture shock signified by feelings of euphoria and excitement

ingroup: a group with whom you associate and consider yourself a member

intercultural communication: communication that occurs specifically between people from two different cultures

intergroup communication: communication between people from two different social, cultural, or demographic groups (such as different ages, genders, or teams)

intergroup interaction: interaction in which communication is driven by each person's respective memberships in various social groups or categories, and not much affected by the unique personal relationships between the people involved

knowledge component: the information you need to know in order to understand how you and others communicate, and what it means to communicate effectively

motivational component: the desire to improve your communication

norms: ideas held by most members of the society about what is appropriate and expected behavior

other-oriented communication: communication in which you consider the needs, goals, desires, and motives of your partner when sending a message

outgroup: a group with whom you have little association and of which you do not consider yourself to be a member

race: the genetically transmitted physical characteristics of a group of people who are classified together

re-entry shock: the stage of culture shock that occurs when the traveler returns to his or her own culture and sees it in a different way, often leading to negative feelings

skills component: the set of behaviors, often learned, that you can employ to improve your communication with others

unconscious competence: when you are so used to using your learned skills that they come naturally

unconscious incompetence: when you are not aware of the deficits in your skill set

CHAPTER 2 ACTIVITIES

Journal

Use this page to respond to the question assigned by your instructor upon completion of this chapter.

Iceberg Model Exercise

Make a list of things about your own culture that might be found in a book for tourists who are visiting.

We wear:

_____

_____

We like:

_____

_____

We are:

_____

_____

We eat:

_____

_____

We don't like:

_____

_____

For fun we:

_____

_____

We value:

_____

_____

To fit in you should:

_____

_____

Now fill in the iceberg for your own culture. List things about your culture that are obvious and visible to visitors above the surface, and things that are subtler under the surface.

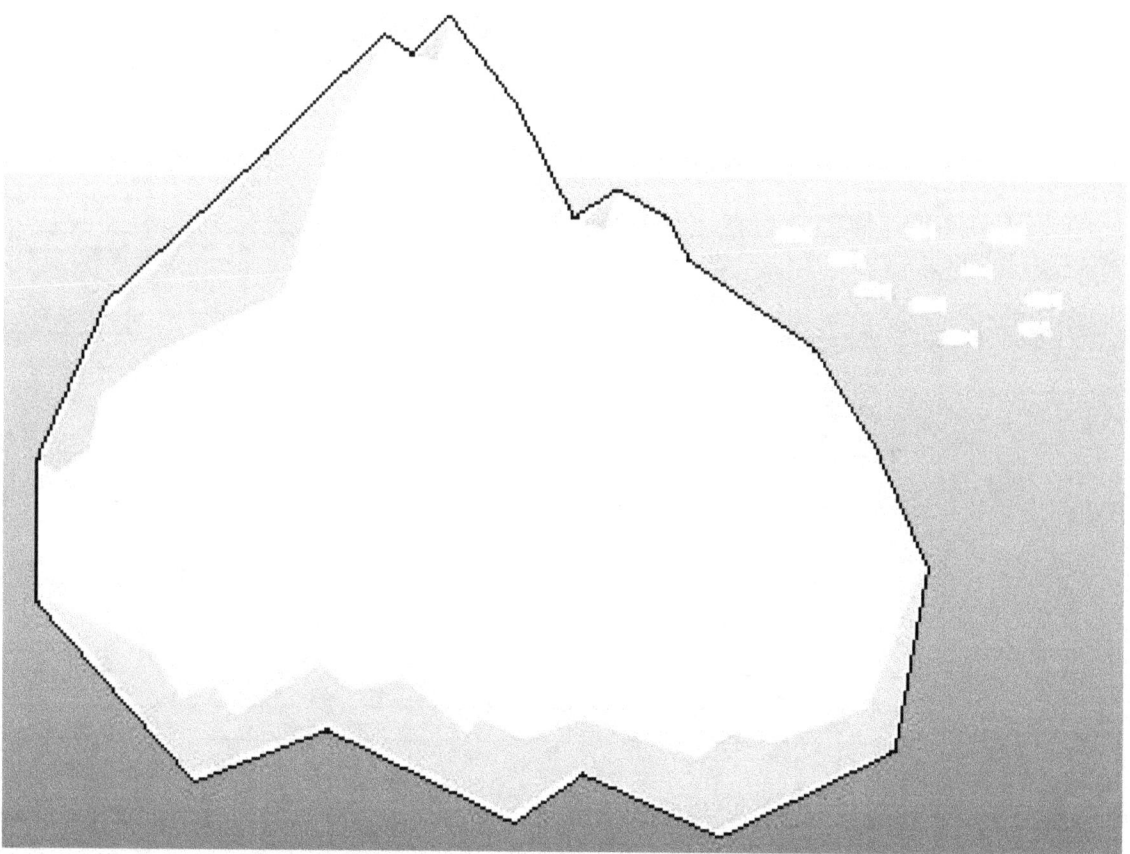

Now make a list of all your cultural observations about another culture:

They wear:

_____
_____
_____

They like:

_____
_____
_____

They are:

_____
_____
_____

They eat:

_____
_____
_____

They don't like:

_____
_____
_____

For fun they:

_____
_____
_____

They value:

_____
_____
_____

To fit in with them you should:

_____
_____
_____

Now fill in the iceberg. List things about this culture that are already obvious and visible to you above the surface, and things that are subtler under the surface.

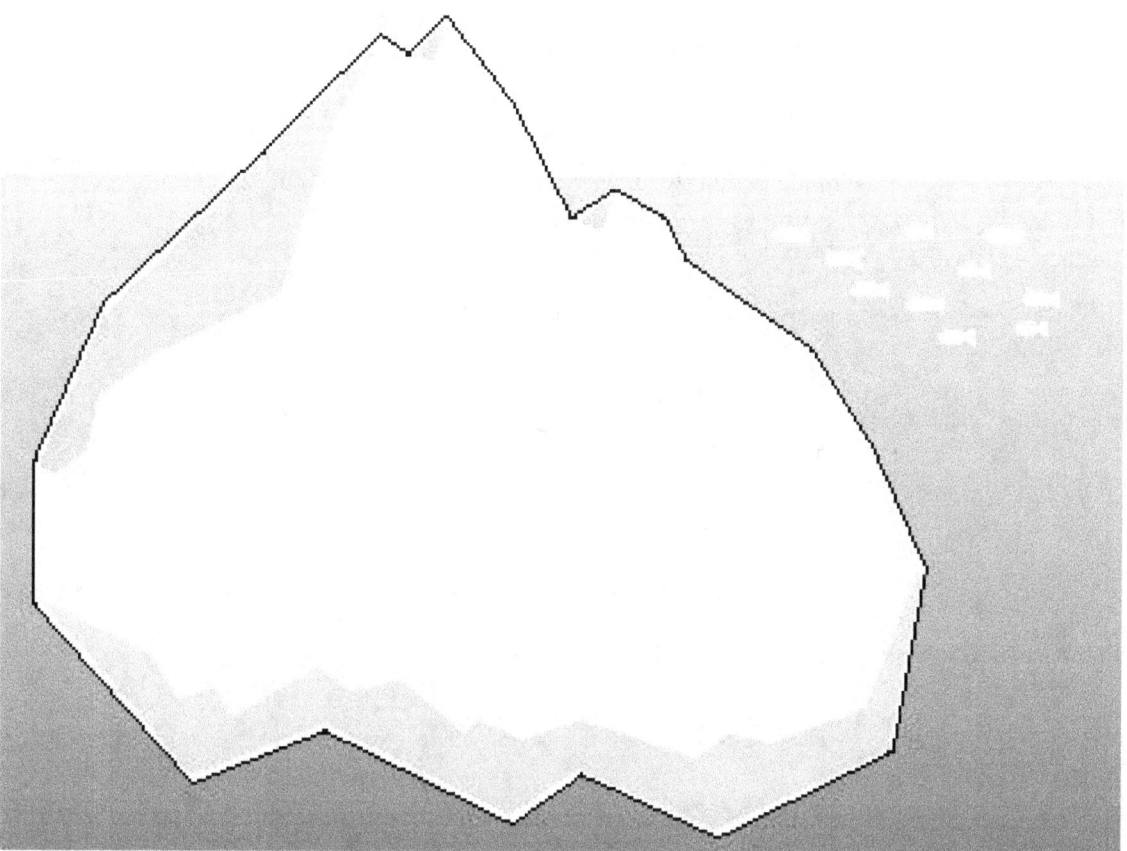

Iceberg Discussion

With a partner from another culture, compare and contrast each of your culture's perspectives on each of the following. Be prepared to share your three most interesting comparisons with the class.

- religious and spiritual beliefs

- the role of government

- child creation (who, when, why) and roles of parents in child raising

- rituals and ceremonies

- food preferences, consumption behaviors

- myths, legends and cultural heroes

- concepts of beauty

- ideas about love

- notions of modesty and appropriateness (style of dress, behavior, etc.)

- ideas about personal space and privacy

- roles of men and women in society

Chapter 3

Verbal and Nonverbal Communication

Learning Objectives

After studying this chapter, you should be able to:

1. Understand the power of words.

2. Describe the impact of culture and identity on word choice.

3. Apply methods for more effective verbal communication in intergroup contexts.

4. Explain the information we derive from nonverbal cues.

5. Describe each channel of nonverbal behavior and examples of cultural variations in each.

Chapter Outline

- Introduction
- The Power of Language
- Culture and Language
- Words Communicate Identity
    - Communication Accommodation Theory
    - Linguistic Intergroup Bias
- Improving Verbal Communication in Intercultural Settings
- The Relationship between Verbal and Nonverbal Communication
- Cultural Norms and Nonverbal Behavior
- Nonverbal Messages
    - Sincerity
    - Interest

Introduction

How many times today did you stop and wonder if the message you were intending to send was the same message someone was receiving? Probably not often, if at all. We tend to operate as if the use of a common language between two people will guarantee "shared meaning," or the same understanding of each other's thoughts. Shared meaning, however, is unfortunately uncommon even when we are speaking the same language.

Interestingly, when you're having a heated argument with someone else it suddenly becomes clear how difficult it is to get your meaning across accurately and efficiently. You may say things that the other person "takes the wrong way," or both people may admit, "I just don't get you!" or "You're not making any sense!" When two people argue, each can see how difficult it is to understand the other, but when things are going well each of us generally assumes that we are being understood even though this is rarely the case. Finnish communication scholar Osmo Wiio (1978) presents several maxims that offer a bleak perspective on finding shared meaning between two people. His maxims state:

1. Communication usually fails, except by accident.
   1.1 If communication can fail, it will.
   1.2 If communication cannot fail, it still most usually fails.
   1.3 If communication seems to succeed in the intended way, there's a

misunderstanding.

2.   If a message can be interpreted in several ways, it will be interpreted in a manner that maximizes the damage.

3.   There is always someone who knows better than you what you meant by your message.

4.   The more we communicate, the faster misunderstandings propagate.

You may be curious about *why* we have such a hard time getting our thoughts back and forth to each other in a way that ensures understanding. This chapter will introduce you to the characteristics of the verbal channel of communication so that you can gain a better understanding of just how complicated it is, *even* when we all speak the same language. Consider the following cultural scenario before we begin:

Jennifer was so excited to live in China for the semester; she could hardly wait to meet her host family. When they picked her up from the airport she could immediately tell they would get along. Her host family had been studying English all year, and Jennifer was the top student in her Chinese class back in the U.S., so it seemed like they would have no trouble communicating. The first night they stayed up until 2 in the morning getting to know each other.

The next night, Jennifer was planning on meeting her American classmates, John and Tom, to compare their first days in China. She got dressed to go out and told her host mother she would be back before 10:00 pm. Her host mother replied, "I think it is too cold for you to go out tonight. Maybe you can meet your friends tomorrow." Jennifer was stunned. Her own mother would never force her to stay home because of the cold. Trying to be respectful, she agreed and called to cancel her meeting with John and Tom.

The next night Jennifer was getting ready to go out again when her host mother entered her room and said "Jennifer, tonight you can help me practice English, it will take many hours since I am so bad at English." Again, Jennifer was surprised because her host mother had said it would be okay for her to go out that night.

The next day during lunch she decided to take another approach and ask in advance. "Would you mind if I met my friends John and Tom tonight? We haven't seen each other since we arrived in China." Her host mother got up to clear the dishes and said "Maybe you would prefer to have them come here tomorrow for lunch." By this time Jennifer had no idea what to think. Did her host mother disapprove of her spending time with other Americans? Was it an expectation that Jennifer would spend every night at home with her host family? What could it be?

After several months in China, Jennifer realized that women don't usually go out alone with two men at night, and this must have been why her host mother kept discouraging her from going out. Why didn't she just say so?

In this chapter you'll learn several characteristics of verbal and nonverbal communication that will help explain the scenario above, including the subtle cultural differences that affect what we say and how we say it.

The Power of Language

Even though words are arbitrary creations that have no meaning other than that which we assign them, once we assign meaning they have enormous power. The meanings we place on words can elicit powerful emotions, cause conflict, and prevent us from seeing things clearly.

We rarely think about how our language shapes what we actually "see" in the world around us. According to the **Sapir-Whorf hypothesis** of Edward Sapir and Benjamin Whorf (1956), words have the power to actually create our reality by limiting how we name and label what we experience. Researcher Deborah Tannen (1990) describes this process, writing:

When we think we are using language, language is using us. ...the terms in which we talk about something shape the way we think about it – and even what we see.

For example, linguists point out that most languages around the world have a disproportionate amount of negative terms to describe the sexually "promiscuous" behavior of women versus that of men. It should come as no surprise, then, that female sexual promiscuity is "viewed" more negatively than male promiscuity: we have more tools with which to describe it as so.

When comparing languages, linguists find that most languages do indeed include some words that have no direct translation to other languages, a phenomenon called **linguistic relativity**. For example, the Swedish word "lagom" does not have an equivalent word in English, and attempts at defining this word seem to fall short. Ask a Swede to tell you the English version of this word and he might say that it means "adequately average" or something similar. You'll quickly realize that the concept doesn't translate to the experience of most U.S. Americans.

It's difficult to find examples of the Sapir-Whorf hypothesis in action because we are too ingrained in our own language to identify it. We use our language without giving it much thought at all, failing to recognize our own role in perpetuating the reality we've created with our words. Take a moment to think about some words from your culture that may have an impact on your experience.

Activity

List as many words you can think of from your native language that do not have a direct or accurate translation to another language:

_____

_____

_____

_____

_____

_____

_____

_____

_____

How do you think these words make your life experience different from that of someone who does not have this word in his or her language?

_____

_____

_____

_____

_____

49

Culture and Language

Culture is a particularly important consideration when choosing how to communicate verbally. As a reminder, culture consists of the rules, norms, and values of a group of people that have been learned, adapted, and passed from one generation to the next. Part of this learned knowledge includes the specific meanings of words, but another part includes *when* and *how* to use language (and when not to use it).

Each culture not only has unique words in its vocabulary, but also has certain rules for how language is used. **Cultural context** is the degree to which meaning is communicated through explicit language or through implicit meanings and nonverbal cues. **High-context cultures** derive most communicative information from nonverbal cues, such as space, eye contact, and body movement. These cultures focus on the connotative meaning of language, or the implied, subtle and relational meaning as opposed to the denotative, or literal meaning. Japan is an example of a country where interactions are based on high-context communication. The desire to "save face," or reduce social embarrassment, is far more important than stating how you feel; thus, people will communicate their messages by using channels other than the verbal channel. When the verbal channel is used, statements are less firm and less assertive than those used by low-context communicators.

In contrast, **low-context cultures** derive most information from the explicitly stated and literal meaning of language, and they tend to pay less attention to subtle information from nonverbal and environmental cues. The United States is an example of a country where low-context communication is the norm. This is shown by such common phrases as "don't beat around the bush," "tell it like it is," and "cut to the chase," which all suggest that efficiency and clarity are important.

One misconception of the difference between high-context and low-context cultures is that high-context cultures are less *direct*. However, high-context cultures are actually no less "direct" than low-context cultures: people raised in a high-context culture understand and use this method of communication with ease. High-context forms of communication may *seem* less direct to people accustomed to communicating in a low-context way, but it's all relative.

When we examine differences in business negotiations between U.S. and Japanese companies we can see a typical example of the difference between high-context and low-context communication norms. Because Japan is a high-context culture, Japanese business people are unlikely to say "no" to a deal because this will cause the other party to lose face, or dignity. Instead, they might say they will discuss it privately, will consider it in the future, or they are not sure. If they were dealing with another Japanese company, both parties would understand that this meant "no." However, U.S. Americans may be confused by what they consider a "wishy-washy" form of negotiating. U.S. business people regularly say "no" as a form of hardball: they welcome competition and are often aggressive when negotiating. Japanese business people have been known to find this method of communication offensive and unnecessary. As shown by this example, the difference between these two cultural contexts lies in the method of getting a point across. The form of communication only becomes problematic when people from high and low-context cultures are trying to communicate with each other!

High-context speech also tends to have more feminine characteristics. There are many ways in which masculine and feminine communication is different. People who use **masculine speech** tend to value achievement and assertiveness, which means they often compete in conversation. In addition, they view communication as information exchange, which has been coined by researcher Deborah Tannen as "report talk." Most masculine individuals base their friendships more on sharing activities than on talking.

In contrast, people who use **feminine speech** use their words to place value on relationships, caring for others, and overall quality of life; thus they are usually supportive rather than competitive in conversation. They often approach communication for the purpose of relating, and to know and be known by others. Tannen terms this type of conversation "rapport talk," because the goal is to build rapport, or closeness, with the other. Feminine speech is also characterized by the use of hedges, disclaimers, and tag questions. Here are some examples of each:

Hedging statement:	"*Maybe* we could call the client?"
Regular statement:	"Let's call the client."
Disclaimer:	"*I might be crazy, but* I don't think they are open on Saturdays."
Regular statement:	"I don't think they are open on Saturdays."
Tag question:	"We're going to wrap up now, *okay*?"
Regular statement:	"We're going to wrap up now."

Activity

If you are not sure whether you are a low-context or high-context communicator, go to: <u>http://www2.pacific.edu/sis/culture/</u>
On the left side menu click 1.4: Whose Fault?
From the expanded menu click 1.4.6: Context of Cultures
Insert your answers and then get your score.

Is your native culture a high-context or low-context culture? Give an example and explain how it contrasts with another culture that is the opposite.

_____
_____
_____
_____
_____
_____
_____
_____
_____
_____
_____
_____
_____
_____

Words Communicate Identity

Have you ever wondered why there isn't a "universal" language? It seems like it would make life so much easier, especially now that international travel and business are so common. Imagine getting off a plane in any country and being able to communicate easily with the natives. Furthermore, if there were a universal tongue you wouldn't have to decide which dreadful language class to suffer through during school. Wouldn't the world's problems be solved much more easily if we could speak the same dialect?

You may be surprised to learn that there is in fact a universal language, and no, it's not English. Esperanto, invented in the late 1870s by Dr. Ludovic Lazarus

Zamenhof, has been coined the world's only universal language. It is estimated that anywhere from 100,000 to 2 million people across the world speak the language fluently. Several organizations use Esperanto as their primary language, there are hundreds of books published in Esperanto, and there are even a few feature-length films where only Esperanto is spoken, including *Incubus*, starring William Shatner. Free lessons are not hard to find; in fact, promoters of the language argue that the average person can reach fluency in a little over two weeks.

If a simple Internet search generates over half a million hits for the term "Esperanto" then why haven't you heard of this universal language? Well, unfortunately the language didn't quite catch on with the contagion its supporters hoped it would. There are various theories for why every global citizen isn't required to learn it, or even inspired to learn it by choice. First of all, the language has been accused of Euro-centrism: its roots are predominately Romantic, and much of the vocabulary and grammar are based on western Indo-European languages. Perhaps an even greater disadvantage of the language is that some people or groups may find it threatening. Verbal communication helps us express our unique identities, which include our memberships in certain groups. Just as groups are attached to their special ways of communicating with ingroup members, countries are attached to their languages and subsets of countries are attached to their particular dialects. We use our unique languages to communicate who we are, and frankly, we don't want to be the same as everyone else. Very few people would willingly *replace* their native tongue with a universal language because it would take away part of their identity.

Communication Accommodation Theory

Using a unique language is not the only way we develop cohesion with ingroup members and distinguish ourselves from outgroups. **Communication accommodation theory** suggests that even when using the same language, people adapt their verbal and nonverbal styles to seem either similar or dissimilar to others, depending on their relationship. If you consider the person with whom you are communicating to be an "ingroup" member, you will engage in **convergence**, which occurs when we choose words and behaviors that match the verbal and nonverbal style of the other person to emphasize similarities. In contrast, if you are communicating with someone whom you consider to be an outgroup member you are likely to engage in **divergence**, which occurs when you differentiate yourself verbally and nonverbally from the other person. Imagine how you speak with a group of your friends. Each of you uses shared words and even vocal tones to convey that you are similar. If you switch contexts and start communicating with your grandmother, chances are you will switch to a more conservative form of speech.

Jargon and slang are two specific tools we use to converge to ingroup members or diverge from outgroup members. **Jargon** is vocabulary that is shared by members of a particular group but that others outside that group may not understand. People often use jargon to demonstrate their knowledge of a subject or membership in a specialized group. When communicating with other members of that special group, jargon can be used to show similarity, understanding, and cohesion. However, jargon can also be used as a tool to alienate outsiders who are not members of a group.

Slang is another type of unique vocabulary used by people who share some kind of group membership. Slang is different from jargon because jargon is usually technical or field-specific, whereas slang is based on similar interests and experience. Slang is also more temporary than jargon; it tends to become popular quickly, then loses popularity over time and eventually becomes extinct.

Slang and jargon make it difficult to master another language. They can also be used as tools to show who is a "real" member of a group, and who is not.

Activity

List and define at least five slang terms from your own languages that a person learning the language would not know or understand:

1. _____
2. _____
3. _____
4. _____
5. _____

Linguistic Intergroup Bias

There are even subtler ways that we communicate our hidden or subconscious biases against outgroups. **Linguistic intergroup bias** is a phenomenon that occurs when positive behavior displayed by an ingroup member is described in relatively *general* terms, whereas the same behavior shown by an outgroup member will be described in relatively *specific* terms. For example, if an ingroup member gives money to a homeless person, we are likely to describe her behavior using a term that generalizes the behavior to her character, such as "Sue is a *generous person*." If an outgroup member gives the same homeless person some money, we are likely to describe her behavior as a specific incident: "Sue *gave* away money." This shows that we see the positive behavior as more enduring and meaningful when it comes from an ingroup member.

The same ingroup preferences are revealed when we describe undesirable behaviors. If an ingroup member strikes someone, we are likely to describe the behavior using specific terms, such as "John *hit* the guy." In contrast, if the person we are describing is an outgroup member, we are more likely to use general character terms such as "John was *violent*." This shows that we excuse the negative behavior when it comes from an ingroup member because it was momentary, whereas the same negative behavior from an outgroup members says something about his or her character. These selective language choices are so subtle and subconscious that when asked, people being studied report that there were no differences in the way they described ingroup versus outgroup members' behavior. We tend to believe we are less biased than we are, but our language reveals the truth about our preferences.

Consider how this Chinese student studying in the U.S. explained his experience with linguistic intergroup bias:

> *I have heard a very famous joke in the U.S. that tells me in the American mind the driver who is from China is very bad. Although it is just a joke, I still think that there are some things we can learn.*

> *There are big differences between Chinese transportation rules and American transportation rules. China has a huge population. As a Chinese driver, you have to get used to driving in chaos. When it comes to the U.S, driving is an entirely different activity. Americans are not as nervous because to them driving is not so dangerous.*

> *Still, when a Chinese driver changes lanes in front of an American, they often say "What a bad Chinese driver." But when an American changes lanes in front of another American, they say "That guy just cut me off." It seems to me like there is a difference in these ways we talk about people from our own culture and people from another culture.*

Improving Verbal Communication in Intercultural Settings

Speaking different languages creates an obvious problem for accurate and clear communication, but issues can exist even when translation is available. Here are a few examples of language blunders posted on Kwintessential.com, a website dedicated to cross-cultural training:

* *Kellogg had to rename its Bran Buds cereal in Sweden when it discovered that the name roughly translated to "burned farmer."*

* *When PepsiCo advertised Pepsi in Taiwan with the ad "Come Alive With Pepsi" they had no idea that it would be translated into Chinese as "Pepsi brings your ancestors back from the dead."*

* *American medical containers were distributed in Great Britain and caused quite a stir. The instructions to "Take off top and push in bottom," innocuous to Americans, had very strong sexual connotations to the British.*

* *In Italy, a campaign for Schweppes Tonic Water translated the name into "Schweppes Toilet Water."*

* *An English sign in a Bangkok dry cleaner's reads: Drop your trousers here for best results.*

* *In an East African newspaper, an English article reads: A new swimming pool is rapidly taking shape since the contractors have thrown in the bulk of their workers.*

* *At a Budapest zoo, a sign says: Please do not feed the animals. If you have any suitable food, give it to the guard on duty.*

These errors could have easily been prevented by having a native speaker proofread the work before publishing or posting it. The difficulties you encounter in foreign settings may be more complex. However, when trying to communicate with outgroup members, there are specific ways to increase effectiveness. Kate Berardo, intercultural trainer and founder of the global resource site Culturosity.com, offers several tips for communicating in situations where one or more participants are not native speakers of the language. These tips also happen to apply to any situation where people from different groups are trying to achieve understanding:

1. Speak slowly and clearly.

Enunciate and slow down your speech. Don't allow time pressures to make you rush important communication. Taking the time to be clear will prevent time you'll have to spend later to correct misunderstandings.

2. Ask for clarification and check for understanding.

Don't be afraid to ask others to repeat themselves. Assuming understanding is the most common communication error people make, even those speaking in their native language. Also ask to make sure others have understood *you.* Use open-ended questions to check other people's understanding instead of using closed questions that simply require a nod. Ask, "What's your understanding of what I just said?" instead of "Is that clear?"

3. Avoid idioms and jargon.

Language is often contextual, and therefore culture specific. U.S. Americans love to use baseball terms such as 'Ballpark figures,' 'Out in left field,' and 'Touch base.' Keep in mind that using a restricted code, or language that requires prior knowledge and common experience, will make communication with a non-native speaker very difficult. Watch the use of acronyms and other jargon that may not be understood by others. If you use them always provide an explanation.

4. Choose your medium of communication effectively.

Experiment with various mediums to see which enhances understanding. If you leave face-to-face interactions feeling confused, try emailing so you have written verification of the message and can spend more time decoding it. Use multiple mediums if necessary, such as sending a follow-up email. Most people report that telephone conversations are difficult in their second language because of the absence of nonverbal cues.

5. Be patient.

Don't expect that communication in a language foreign to you will be as easy as communication between two native speakers. Assume that it will take time, and enter into communication situations with patience.

When it comes to understanding each other, nonverbal communication is just as important, if not more important, than verbal communication. The next section will introduce you to the channel of nonverbal communication, which can carry up to 90% of the meaning of a message.

The Relationship between Verbal and Nonverbal Communication

Many people use the term "body language" as synonymous with nonverbal communication, but nonverbal communication is much more complex than this.

Consider this example:

> *In his popular book Outliers, author Malcom Gladwell explains how certain verbal and nonverbal norms can have dire consequences. To support his "Ethnic Theory of Plane Crashes" he describes startling statistics about the frequency of plane crashes in cultures where there exists both high power distance (characterized by respect for and submission to authority figures) and high uncertainty avoidance (characterized by the inability to critique and question rules of conduct). Gladwell argues that pilots are significantly more likely to make bad decisions in a cockpit where 1) the co-pilot who is subordinate is not supposed to question the captain, and b) rules and regulations supersede common sense and critical thinking. Gladwell explains that members of high power distance and high uncertainty cultures are more likely to use something called "mitigated speech," or language that is tentative in order not to offend superiors. Thus, in cultures where authority and rules go unquestioned, a co-pilot will not correct the errors of a captain. Using evidence of historical plane crashes by means of flight*

recordings, Gladwell demonstrates that flights where the co-pilot was in the "flying seat" and the captain was checking for errors were much less likely to crash because the captain (as the figure of authority) spoke up. Yet when the captain was in the "flying seat" his obvious errors went unquestioned by his subordinate, the co-pilot; there might as well have only been one person in the cockpit. Gladwell concludes that in high power distance and high uncertainty avoidance cultures, "planes are safer when the least experienced pilot is flying because it means the second pilot isn't going to be afraid to speak up." (p.197)

This example illustrates how the concepts we just covered in the verbal communication section are inextricably linked with nonverbal communication behaviors. **Nonverbal communication** is any communicative behavior other than written or spoken language that creates meaning for someone. It makes sense with this broad definition that nonverbal behaviors comprise the majority of our messages. Communication theorists have tried to account for the specific percentage of meaning derived from the verbal and nonverbal channels; Mehrabian (1972) concluded that as little as 7% of the meaning of our messages is communicated explicitly through verbal channels, which means that up to 93% is communicated nonverbally. Although the exact percentage is uncertain, scholars unanimously agree that the *majority* of our messages come through nonverbal channels.

Nonverbal messages work with verbal messages to create meaning, and each plays an equally important role in constructing effective communication messages. First, nonverbal cues help us manage verbal messages by *regulating* them. For example, when you have something to say you may engage in several nonverbal behaviors that indicate your desire to speak, such as opening your mouth, clearing your throat, or even putting up your hand. In addition, nonverbal cues can *emphasize* or *support* verbal messages. When someone uses a hand to show a child's height while describing him, he or she is emphasizing the verbal message with a nonverbal gesture. Nonverbal messages can also *contradict* a verbal message. When your friend insists, "Nothing's wrong," but she has a scowl on her face, the verbal and nonverbal messages are contradictory. Finally, nonverbal cues can *replace* verbal messages. When you don't know the answer to someone's question you might simply shrug instead of responding verbally, which means you have replaced verbal communication with a nonverbal response.

Another way in which nonverbal and verbal messages differ is that nonverbal messages are continuous. Words are discrete entities that have a beginning and an end; that is, we can easily point out when someone is talking and when they are not. In contrast, nonverbal cues occur in a continuous stream that has no set beginning and end, so they are difficult to categorize and interpret. You may stop using your tone of voice, but all the while you are still gesturing. And once you stop gesturing, you are still communicating nonverbally through your posture, use of space, and what you are wearing. As such, there is no end to your nonverbal communication.

An additional reason why nonverbal messages are distinct is that nonverbal cues are multi-channeled; they come from a variety of sources simultaneously. Although you develop an overall "impression" of the message being delivered through the combination of channels, you can only actually attend to one nonverbal cue at a time when you are trying to categorize them. This may explain why nonverbal messages speak more "loudly" than messages from the verbal channel; there are more channels occurring at once and therefore there is more information, even when we cannot pinpoint exactly where it is coming from.

By now, nonverbal communication may seem quite complicated. One way to better understand and utilize nonverbal communication in intergroup and intercultural settings is to analyze it according to the sub-channels, or categories of nonverbal cues. The next section will highlight the various categories of nonverbal communication so that you can better understand your own and other's nonverbal messages.

Cultural Norms and Nonverbal Behavior

The culture in which you were born and raised has an enormous impact on the meaning you assign to nonverbal cues. **Display rules** are the implicit rules we use to measure the appropriateness of different nonverbal behaviors, and each group has its own rules. For example, it is a commonly understood "rule" in many Central and South American cultures that strong emotional displays are encouraged. However, in many Asian cultures emotional displays are considered inappropriate. Unfortunately, we are often unaware of the display rules of cultures other than our own, so nonverbal misperceptions are common in intercultural communication settings. U.S. President Barack Obama offers a recent example of nonverbal misperception during his visit to Japan. Critics claimed his bow to Japan's Emperor Akihito was too low, and sent a message of powerlessness and deference to Japan.

Cultural groups are not the only types of groups that have norms and expectations for nonverbal behavior. We find different behaviors across genders as well, which will be covered in an upcoming section. Learning more about how we communicate nonverbally can get us closer to shared meaning even in intercultural, intergender, and other intergroup interactions, so let's take a look at some specific information we decode from nonverbal messages.

Nonverbal Messages

As you've learned, nonverbal communication is particularly revealing because it is a *less conscious* reflection of one's attitude toward others, often expressing perceptions that are not decipherable from more controlled verbal communication. When we're in doubt about what someone *really* means, we pay attention to his or her nonverbal behavior. We derive some specific information from nonverbal behavior that we cannot always tell by focusing on words alone, including sincerity, interest, and dominance.

Sincerity

In both high-context and low-context cultures, nonverbal messages are more believable than verbal messages. We have learned through experience that people do not always say what they mean, and we often think that we can detect the truth if we pay close attention to **leakage cues**, or nonverbal behaviors that indicate someone might be lying. This idea has been especially popular in the research on deception. Unfortunately, it is very difficult to become an expert in decoding deception for several reasons. First, good liars often know which nonverbal cues to control, which they have conveniently learned from experience. For example, U.S. American children were told by their mothers "Look me in the eye to show me you aren't lying." In other cultures, parents teach their children to show honesty and sincerity by looking away because direct eye contact is considered disrespectful. Either way, each person knows which lying cues they should control if they want to be believable.

The second reason it is difficult to "decode" nonverbal lying behavior is that we are usually only good at detecting dishonesty from people we know because we sense when their behavior is different from normal; we have no foundation for what is normal for people we don't know and could easily mistake their normal behavior for lying, or their lying behavior for truth. This is especially true when we are interacting with an outgroup member. We often misunderstand nonverbal cues from outgroup members because nonverbal behaviors are not universal: the same behavior may mean different things in different cultures.

Finally, people are so unique that each individual's leakage cues are different. Some people might tend to include too many details when they are lying, others will say "um" too much (again, another reason why knowing the "normal" behavior of the person helps). Because of our personal idiosyncrasies, there is no dictionary of nonverbal behavior that we can study to detect lying in all situations.

Interest

In addition to our use of nonverbal cues to detect sincerity and honesty, we use them to detect friendliness and approachability. **Immediacy cues** are behaviors that communicate liking and show feelings of pleasure. We gravitate toward people and things we like and nonverbally move away from those we dislike. People pick up on these cues and they can have an enormous impact on how we perceive one another.

There are several dimensions of immediacy, and they vary across cultures. In the United States, *involvement* is indicated by directness of gaze and body orientation, closer distance, and positive feedback, such as nodding of the head and smiling. *Pleasantness*, is the level of attentiveness, receptiveness, and adaptability toward the other during conversation. In the United States pleasantness is communicated through a warm and friendly voice and interested body orientation. *Expressiveness* is the degree to which communicators are dynamic and animated. U.S. Americans are especially known (and sometimes critiqued) for their emotional expressiveness. In the United States, nonverbal behaviors that elicit positive evaluations of expressiveness include facial and gestural animation.

According to a research study conducted by Fons Trompenaars in 1998, other emotionally expressive cultures include (in order of expressiveness):

- Mexico
- Brazil

- Italy
- Venezuela
- Spain

In contrast, some of the least expressive countries found in the same study included (in order of lowest expressiveness):

- Japan
- United Kingdom
- Singapore
- Australia
- Indonesia
- Hong Kong
- Belgium
- Germany
- Sweden

Dominance

Finally, **dominance cues** communicate status, position, importance, and control. U.S. Americans communicate dominance through the increased use of space, more direct eye contact, initiating touch, increased vocal volume, lower pitch and greater pitch range, and increased interruptions. Dominant body orientation can include pointing, hovering over the other, standing with hands on hips, and an expanded chest. U.S. Americans often avoid dominance cues when they like someone because they want to send a message of equality (reflect back on President Obama's bow).

There are certain cues that may be perceived as dominant by someone from another culture, but are actually gestures of friendship in the U.S. such as a slap on the back, a firm handshake, or grabbing of the other's shoulders or arm. In many Asian cultures, such as Japan, these behaviors would be considered aggressive and dominant.

Categories of Nonverbal Behavior

The Body

Human movement, posture, and gesture comprise a large category of nonverbal behavior. Gestures in particular are divided into the following additional categories.

Emblems are bodily cues – often in the form of hand gestures – that have a specific and commonly understood meaning in a given culture and may even substitute for a word or phrase. The "peace" sign (✌) is an example of an emblem. Note, however, that this emblem is culturally relative, which is typical of emblems; they usually mean something different depending on the culture in which they are used. This particular emblem can actually be quite offensive in some cultures, signifying a derogatory slur or insult. Other emblems that are culturally relative include the "thumbs-up" sign (👍) and the "a-okay" sign (👌). Make sure you ask the meaning of these gestures before you use them on foreign soil!

Another category of bodily cues called **illustrators** are nonverbal behaviors that accompany a verbal message and either contradict, accent, or complement it. A typical example of an illustrator is when someone uses their hands to emphasize the words "this big," (for example, in describing the fish you caught, or slice of pie you ate).

Adaptors are bodily cues that help people adapt to a situation by channeling excess energy, such as excitement or nervousness, through a bodily movement. When someone taps a pencil on his desk or twirls her hair, they are using adaptors. Adaptors are often habitual, meaning we tend to select a particular behavior and repeat it. Think for a moment about what adaptors you use when you have too much energy or anxiety, such as when you are delivering a presentation in front of the class.

Regulators are nonverbal messages that help to control the flow of communication between people during an interaction. In the U.S. classroom, it is typical to raise your hand to ask a question, but in personal interactions you may use other cues to regulate the conversation such as opening your mouth as if ready to speak, furrowing your brow when you'd like to express that you are about to disagree, or leaning forward to show you have something to contribute.

India has a regulator entirely unique to Indian culture, affectionately referred to as the "head bobble." This motion of the head is somewhere between a nod for "yes" and a shake for "no," and the meaning is rather difficult for foreigners to understand.

Finally, **affect displays** are nonverbal bodily behaviors that communicate emotion. Emotion can come through a combination of nonverbal channels, such as the way you walk, hold your arms, or posture yourself. We pay special attention to affect displays, whether consciously or unconsciously, because they tell us how someone is feeling.

The Face

The head and face are obviously a part of the body, but in the United States this channel is so expressive that it deserves a category of its own, called **facial cues**. Your face is capable of producing over 250,000 different expressions, according to researchers Ekman and Friesen (1969). These scholars tested the universality of emotional expression by showing pictures of various expressions to people all over the world, asking them what emotion was signified by the expression they were seeing. From their studies they concluded that six expressions are recognized universally: sadness, anger, disgust, fear, surprise, and happiness. As you learned earlier, cultures vary in their level of expressiveness of these emotions. For example, members of collectivistic cultures are often encouraged to show less emotion through their facial expressions because they are encouraged not to stand out, while individualist cultures tend to value facial animation and expressiveness because it shows individuality.

Perhaps the most expressive part of the face is the eye area. Not only does the shape we make with our eyes reveal a great deal about how we're feeling, but we can also communicate strong messages by using or avoiding eye contact with another person. Again, this nonverbal channel is extremely culturally relative. In U.S. culture we often interpret direct eye contact as exuding confidence and sincerity, yet in many cultures direct eye contact is considered threatening or offensive. In most Muslim cultures eye contact depends on gender; men are not supposed to look women in the eye for prolonged periods, if at all. Some Native American groups believe that someone can steal the soul of another person by looking him directly in the eyes. Countries with greater power distance such as Japan and China engage in less direct eye contact, especially toward a superior or elder.

Distance

The space we keep between us communicates our relationship with another person, our interactive goals, and the spatial norms of our culture. For example, some Middle Eastern cultures believe that two communicators should be close enough to smell each other's breath. Standing too far apart may indicate something is wrong in the relationship.

Edward Hall (1963) identified four zones that people in Western cultures use to define their relationships with others.

- **Intimate space** is the zone of space most often reserved for intimate interactions, and it ranges from 0-1.5 feet from the individual (metric: between touching and about ½ meter).

- **Personal space** is the zone of space normally used in a conversation with friends, families, colleagues, and even sometimes strangers, which ranges from 1.5 to 4 feet from the individual (metric: between about a ½ meter and 1.25 meters)

- **Social space** is the zone of distance typically used during group interactions, ranging from four feet to twelve feet (metric: between 1.25 and a bit under 6 meters)

- **Public space** is the distance most often used in one-to-many interactions, such as public speaking, which extends twelve feet or more from the individual (metric: between 6 meters and beyond).

The spatial zones you find comfortable may also have to do with your unique personality. U.S Americans refer to their individual tolerance for closeness with others as their "personal bubble." Think about the size of your personal bubble and how that affects your interactions with others.

Touch

Another nonverbal channel through which we communicate meaning is through touch. We use touch to emphasize our words, to communicate affection, to assert ourselves or dominate others, and to manage interactions. Each individual has a different tolerance and need for touch, just as we each have a differently sized "personal bubble." You probably have friends whom you consider very affectionate, and others who are noticeably "stand offish" when it comes to touch.

In addition to personal differences in our preferences for touch, certain cultures are more "touchy." Research indicates that Italians, Greeks, and Brazilians engage in more conversational touching than any other culture, while British citizens are cited as engaging in the least amount of touch.

Culture norms for the handshake are especially diverse. In some cultures is it customary to shake with only one hand, while others prefer a shake with two hands (one hand on the wrist of the other person). In some Islamic cultures, men and women who are not intimately related are not supposed to have any form of physical contact, including a handshake. Cultures also vary in their interpretation of the firmness of the handshake: U.S. Americans prefer a firm grip, while Japanese prefer what Americans interpret as a "cold fish" handshake (gentle and soft). The length of the hand embrace also sends different messages in different cultures: U.S. Americans tend to let go more quickly, and holding onto the hand may be considered too intimate. Other cultures may hold on for up to 30 seconds and letting go too soon may indicate that you are not trustworthy. Of course, many cultures do not shake hands at all, but instead use other forms of greeting such as a bow.

Appearance and Artifacts

Appearance serves as yet another category in the nonverbal channel. U.S. American culture places a high value upon how much people weigh, the style of their hair, and the clothes they wear. One part of appearance is **artifacts**, which includes anything in addition to your own physical body that communicates something about you. Artifacts can include jewelry, a cell phone, a car, your purse, backpack, hat, or any other item you use or wear. Critical to understanding the role of artifacts is remembering that not all messages you send are intentional, and not all of the messages people interpret about you are accurate. Nonetheless, one of the reasons nonverbal communication is continuous is because we all display artifacts, almost all of the time.

The Voice

Vocal cues are the final and perhaps most misunderstood category among the nonverbal channels. Just because vocal cues come out of your mouth does not mean they are considered verbal. Remember, verbal communication is based on words and language. Vocal cues include the tone, speed, pitch, and volume of your words. In sum, vocal cues are anything having to do with "how" you say what you say. As you are probably aware, *how* you say your message carries a lot more meaning than *what* you say. You can communicate any emotion with just a small inflection of your voice, including anger, disgust, sarcasm, excitement, confusion, and infinitely more. Out loud, communicate each of the listed emotions using the same sentence:

Showing anger, say: "I love it when you do that."

Showing disgust, say: "I love it when you do that."

Showing nostalgia, say: "I love it when you do that."

Showing excitement, say: "I love it when you do that."

As you can see, we are well equipped to greatly vary the meaning of our message simply by adjusting our vocal cues. One of the most difficult parts of learning to speak a second language is learning to use vocal cues like the natives do. Each language has a unique way of using intonation, accentuation, and emphasis. Even if you speak your second language with very little detectable accent, your intonation may be different than a native speaker.

Activity

Describe one difference between the nonverbal behaviors of your own culture and those of another culture in each of the following channels:

body movement (gestures, posture)

_____

_____

_____

facial cues

_____

_____

_____

distance

_____

_____

_____

touch

_____

_____

_____

appearance

_____

_____

_____

artifacts

_____

_____

_____

vocal cues

_____

_____

_____

Gender and Nonverbal Communication

Research indicates that there are several categories of nonverbal behavior that are especially prone to differences in the ways they are used by men and women, but even these norms vary across cultures:

- Distance:
    - When it comes to space in the U.S. women tend to sit or stand more closely to others, and both sexes approach women more closely than they approach men. Men tend to use more space, which can be attributed to space as a function of relative power: because men have traditionally had more power in society, they have become accustomed to taking up more space.
    - In Muslim cultures men and women do not sit or stand close to each other unless they are in a crowded space. Men stand much closer to other men, and women closer to other women.

- Eye contact:
    - In their use of eye contact, U.S. American women are more likely to prolong their gaze during conversation in a way that communicates affiliation, but men are more likely to use eye contact as a form of power through staring or glaring.
    - In many other cultures such as those found in Saudi Arabia and China, women are not supposed to use prolonged gaze with men or it is considered a sexual invitation. Averting one's eyes shows respect and modesty.

- Facial expression:
    - In the U.S. women tend to smile more than men, and their facial expressions tend to be more expressive overall (they are also a little better at interpreting people's expressions, particularly negative ones such as anger).

- Touch:
    - When it comes to touch, U.S. American women are less likely than men to initiate it, but they use it more often to communicate support

and warmth. Men are more likely to use touch to demonstrate power or status.

- In Brazil, touch between men and women is common, and kissing upon greeting is a cultural expectation.
- In Turkey and Saudi Arabia, men often link arms or hold hands while walking.
- In Japan, women often link arms or hold hands while walking.

- Vocal cues:
  - Women all over the world tend to speak at a higher pitch and a softer volume than men. Although some of this pitch variance can be attributed to women having a smaller larynx, it has been suggested that women who live in less egalitarian cultures tend to have even higher vocal pitch than normal, and that the more a culture focuses on youth and femininity the more likely it is that the women will intentionally speak more like children than adults.

Simplifying Verbal and Nonverbal Decoding

That's a lot of information to remember about nonverbal communication! If you feel overwhelmed keep in mind that an overall understanding of the concepts presented throughout this text can help you know what is appropriate in any given group. Remembering each of these tips can help you communicate more successfully, especially when it comes to intercultural interactions:

- Cultures can be categorized by whether they are verbally direct (low-context), or verbally indirect (high-context) and those that are direct use more powerful and expressive nonverbal behavior.

- Cultures differ in their levels of individualism and collectivism: collectivistic cultures use fewer nonverbal behaviors that would make them stand out, such as facial expressions and dramatic gestures.

- Cultures can be classified by whether they are high power distance (deference to authority and rules) or low power distance (egalitarian). Those that are high power distance have stricter and more conservative rules for nonverbal behavior between people of different statuses, and between men and women

- Cultures can be understood according to their comfort with uncertainty, and cultures with high uncertainty avoidance usually have stricter rules for nonverbal behavior.

Using these generalizations about nonverbal norms will allow you to get in the right frame of mind for the group in which you are interacting. If all else fails, you can ask someone what you should do! Chances are, he or she will respect your concern for his or her values and appreciate your effort.

Chapter Summary

The verbal communication channel is used when we utilize language to translate our thoughts to people around us. In intercultural relationships it is especially difficult to decode the intended meaning of another person's ideas because of the arbitrary nature of language: words have no meaning outside of the meaning we assign them. Communication is further complicated by the enormous power that our words have, and their ability to shape the way we experience the world. The Sapir-Whorf Hypothesis suggests that we are prisoners of our language in that we can't really experience things we don't have the words to describe. The cultural context in which the communication occurs also creates a challenge due to differences in high-context and low-context language, and the differences between masculine and feminine communication.

The nonverbal channels include any non-linguistic form of communication. Nonverbal communication differs from verbal communication in that it is continuous and multi-channeled, making it harder to study but even more communicative than verbal messages. The various categories of nonverbal behavior were outlined to show how complex nonverbal communication is, including bodily cues, facial cues, distance, touch, appearance and artifacts, and the voice. The information we derive from nonverbal cues includes sincerity, interest, and dominance. However, all information we perceive depends on our own gender and culture: nonverbal norms vary greatly between people who are either masculine or feminine communicators, and especially those from different cultural backgrounds.

Key Terms

adaptors: kinetic behaviors that help a person to adapt to situation by channeling their energy, such as excitement or nervousness, through a bodily movement

affect displays: nonverbal behaviors that communicate emotion

appearance: a category in the nonverbal channels that describes communication through how you look

artifacts: anything in addition to your own physical body that communicates something about you

communication accommodation theory: a theory that suggests that people adapt their verbal and nonverbal styles to seem either similar or dissimilar to the person with whom they are interacting

convergence: communication behavior that occurs when we accommodate to be similar to the verbal and nonverbal style of the person with whom we are interacting to emphasize our similarities

cultural context: the degree to which meaning is communicated through explicit language or through nonverbal cues

display rules: the implicit rules we use to measure the appropriateness of different nonverbal behaviors, and each group has its own rules

divergence: communication behaviors that occur when you differentiate yourself verbally and nonverbally from the person with whom you are interacting

dominance cues: nonverbal behaviors that communicate status, position, importance, and control

emblems: bodily cues, often in the form of hand gestures, that have a specific and commonly understood meaning in a given culture and may even substitute for a word or phrase

facial cues: the channel of nonverbal behavior from which you are able to communicate by producing over 250,000 different expressions

feminine speech: using language that is supportive rather than competitive in conversation; feminine speakers approach communication for the purpose of relating, and to know and be known by others

high-context cultures: cultures that derive most communicative information from nonverbal cues, such as space, eye contact, and body movement

illustrators: nonverbal behaviors that accompany a verbal message and either contradict, accent, or complement it

immediacy cues: nonverbal behaviors that communicate liking and show feelings of pleasure

intimate space: the zone of personal space most often reserved for personal or intimate interactions, ranging from zero to one and one-half feet from the individual

jargon: vocabulary that is shared by members of a particular group, but that others outside that group may not understand

leakage cues: nonverbal behaviors that indicate someone might be lying

nonverbal communication: any communicative behavior other than written or spoken language that creates meaning for someone

linguistic intergroup bias: a phenomenon that occurs when positive behavior displayed by an ingroup member is described in relatively *general* terms, whereas the same behavior shown by an outgroup member will be described in relatively *specific* terms (and vice versa)

linguistic relativity: the idea that each language includes some unique features that are not contained in other languages

low-context cultures: cultures that derive much information from the literal, or denotative meaning words, and they tend to pay less attention to information from nonverbal and environmental cues

masculine speech: language that shows assertiveness, often characterized by competitive conversation style

personal space: the zone of personal space normally used in a conversation with friends, families, colleagues, and even sometimes strangers, which ranges from one and one-half to four feet from the individual

public space: the distance most often used in a one-to-many interaction, such as public speaking, which extends twelve feet or more from the individual

regulators: nonverbal messages that help to control the flow of communication between people during an interaction

Sapir-Whorf hypothesis: a perspective that is based on the principles of linguistic determinism and linguistic relativity, suggesting that the words we select and use create the world we see around us

slang: unique vocabulary used by people who share a group membership

social space: the zone of personal space typically used during group interactions, ranging from four feet to twelve feet

CHAPTER 3 ACTIVITIES

Journal

Use this page to respond to the question assigned by your instructor upon completion of this chapter.

_____

_____

_____

_____

_____

_____

_____

_____

_____

_____

_____

_____

_____

_____

_____

_____

_____

_____

_____

_____

_____

_____

_____

_____

_____

_____

_____

_____

_____

_____

_____

_____

_____

_____

_____

_____

New Slang Words

Interview your classmates to find at least five slang terms from different languages and list them here with their definitions:

1._____
2._____
3._____
4._____
5._____

High/Low Context Communication

Interview your classmates to determine which countries are high context and which are low context. List them here:

High Context Countries   Low Context Countries

_____   _____
_____   _____
_____   _____
_____   _____
_____   _____

Distance and Space Exercise

Imagine that the picture below is a passport checkpoint at the airport. There are eight patrons about to enter the room to get their passports stamped. Place the circles below to represent how the people would arrange themselves in order to be helped by the person at the counter

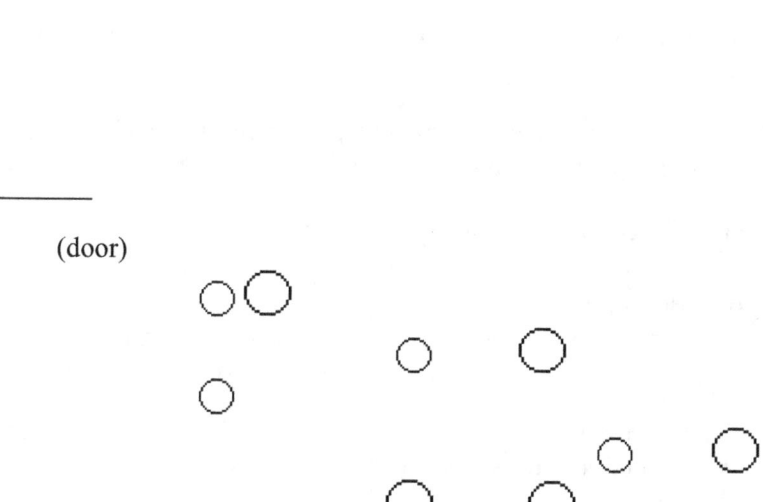

(door)

Chapter 4

Intercultural Perception

Learning Objectives

After studying this chapter, you should be able to:

1. Describe the five cultural value dimensions and how they impact worldview.

2. Describe the stages of perception and identify errors that occur in each stage.

3. Understand the consequences of perceptual distortion, including stereotyping, prejudice and discrimination.

4. Apply strategies for more accurate perceptions.

Chapter Outline

- Introduction
- The Self-Concept
  - Attitudes, Values, and Beliefs
- Worldview
- Cultural and Worldview
  - High/Low Uncertainty Avoidance
  - High/Low Power Distance
  - Individualism/Collectivism
  - Long Term/Short Term Time Orientation
  - Masculine/Feminine Orientation
- Communicating Across Worldviews

Introduction

After Professor Smith took attendance on the first day of class she answered student questions about the course and the syllabus. One American student raised her hand and asked,

"What would you like us to call you?"

"Please call me by my first name, which is Joan," the professor replied.

Kano, an international student from Japan, was surprised by her classmate's directness. She knew that American students often call their professors by their first names, but was very surprised that the student came right out and asked the professor what to do. Kano worried that this could have been very embarrassing for the professor, and she felt like it made the student look foolish. Kano resolved that she would be much more polite and always use the professor's title just to be safe.

After class that day Kano approached the professor saying, "Professor Smith, I have a question about the syllabus."

Her professor answered the question, and followed by saying, "By the way, you should ask your questions out loud in class in case another student has the same question. And please call me Joan."

The next class session a similar situation occurred. Kano approached Joan after class about a point from the lecture.

"Professor Smith, could you please give me an example of what you mean by 'theory'?"

Joan answered her question but followed by again saying, "Kano, I really want you to speak up in class when we are discussing the topic about which you have a question. It will benefit everyone and help your participation score. And again, please call me Joan."

On the third day of class when Kano approached the professor again, still refusing to use her first name, Joan was frustrated. She felt like Kano was not very good at listening and perhaps not very intelligent, either.

What went wrong here? Why are both communicators unable to meet each other's needs and get their message across at the same time? This situation is more common than most people realize. Achieving shared meaning is difficult enough when communicating with someone you know well. When it comes to communicating with outgroup members, shared meaning is nearly impossible unless you learn about some of the fundamental differences in the way you and your communication partner perceive the world. In this chapter you will learn about your self-concept to give you a better idea of the lens through which you view the world around you. Then, you'll learn about how your culture contributes to your perceptions and what you can do about it.

The Self-Concept

The famous psychologist Carl Jung once said: "Everything that irritates us about others can lead us to an understanding of ourselves." Knowing about ourselves is key in our process of understanding other people, especially those from other groups. It makes sense, then, that our education about other cultures should start with a look at our own selves, and our own culture.

Self is defined as the sum total of who a person is; it is the place from which all thoughts stem, and consequently all communication. Your **self-concept** is your idea of this self; it is your subjective personal description of who you think you are. This description has an enormous impact on how you interact with the world around you and communicate with others.

Attitudes, Values, and Beliefs

We show others the many parts of our selves by expressing how we feel about the world around us. One of these expressions takes the form of our **attitudes**, which are favorable or unfavorable predispositions to a person, situation, or thing. Attitudes are usually expressed as a like or dislike for something, such as, "I dislike Korean food." **Beliefs** are concepts of what is true and what is false. Examples of beliefs include, "I believe there is a life after death," or "I believe in God." **Values** are enduring concepts of good and bad, or right and wrong, such as, "Lying is wrong." Values are essentially your moral standards.

Attitudes, values, and beliefs are socialized concepts, meaning you learn them starting at an early age and they are reinforced throughout your upbringing. Attitudes are more individualistic than beliefs and values, since your preferences may change with time and age. However, beliefs and values have a lot to do with your culture because it is your culture that produces your systems of thought. Beliefs and values are *culturally relative*, meaning that each culture has a different set of ideas about what is true and false, right and wrong. For example, some cultures value the principle of "an eye for an eye," and they enforce this value by ordering thieves to have their hands cut off; other cultures consider these laws to be inhumane and barbaric. Beliefs and values are usually ingrained, which means they are so much a part of our fabric that they feel natural, and we have a hard time seeing the validity of any perspective outside of our own system of thought.

Culturally relative concepts that are deeply ingrained create a special problem for people communicating across cultures. It is especially difficult to adapt to and respect people from another culture when your own beliefs and values are in conflict with theirs. Coping with different systems of thought is one of the greatest challenges in intercultural communication.

Worldview

In addition to your own personal identity, you also have a cultural identity. When your parents were raising you, you were taught how to understand the world around you in the form of lessons and beliefs that come from your culture. This overall understanding of the world creates filters through which you eventually view all new life experiences, and these filters combine to form your "worldview." **Worldview** is derived from the German word *Weltanschauung*, meaning to "look onto the world." Your worldview is the framework through which you interpret the world, including everyone you meet and everything that happens to you.

Worldview is usually comprised of several elements:

- Your worldview includes an **ontology**, which is a descriptive model of the world and its parts or inhabitants. Your notion of the relationships between humans, nature, animals, and spirits are part of your ontology.

- Your worldview also includes an **explanation** of the world around you. This includes answers to questions such as "How does the world operate?" and "What are the principles of its functioning?"

- A **futurology** is also included in your worldview, which is a concept of where the world is headed. Science fiction movies that provide an outlook on the future, especially apocalyptic movies, demonstrate a futurology.

- **Ethical standards** are inevitably a part of your worldview. These are values that help you answer the questions "What *should* be done?"

- In most worldviews you will also find a **methodology**, or theory of action that directs us on how to attain goals. For example, does a happy life come from hard work or good fortune?

- Also integral to a worldview is an **etiology**, or account of the world's origins and constructions. Did God create the world instantly, or did humans evolve?

Activity

How would you describe your country's worldview to a visitor? Explain each of the following about your country:

Ontology: This is what we believe about the role of humans, animals, and nature on this planet:

_____

_____

_____

Explanation: This is what we believe about "how life is" (random, luck, predetermined, determined by karma, etc.)

_____

_____

_____

Futurology: This is what we believe about the future of the world:

_____

_____

_____

Ethical standards: This is what we believe is right and wrong:

_____

_____

_____

Methodology: This is how we believe you should reach your goals:

_____

_____

_____

Etiology: This is what we believe about how the world and humans were created:

_____

_____

_____

Worldviews are often shared by geographic groups of people because their life experience is composed of similar social systems and language. People from completely different areas of the world tend to have different experiences, and therefore different worldviews. Consequently our beliefs about what is true, real, and right overlap in some ways, but not in others. When communicating with another person we often assume that he or she sees the world in the same way as we do, when in reality we may be coming from different schools of thought. This presents a special challenge for achieving shared meaning and communicating effectively.

To exemplify the strength of worldview, consider the cultural differences between India and the U.S. when it comes to perceptions of social status. The United States was founded upon the concept of equal opportunity for all people, as stated in the constitution, "with liberty and justice for all." Many people would argue about whether or not equal opportunity is a reality in the United States, but few would argue that the same opportunities exist elsewhere. India's history includes the development of a more clearly defined system of social stratification, known as the caste system. Although this system was technically outlawed in 1950, experts argue that it still plays a major role in Indian society. According to the laws of this system, the caste into which one is born determines the profession he or she can pursue, ranging from prestigious government jobs to manual labor and sanitation jobs. One's caste can also determine whom he or she marries, and with whom he or she can socialize. A group known as The Untouchables (referred to by Mahatma Gandhi as "Harijans") represents the lowest caste, and are generally considered to be sub-human; most members of other castes ignore people born into the Untouchables caste. Although it is now illegal to discriminate based on this system, this practice is difficult to abolish because a person's caste is indicated by his or her last name. The belief that people are born into their destiny therefore remains a fundamental belief in the worldview of many Indians.

Although worldviews differ from region to region and from person to person, there are some values that appear in nearly every culture around the world, one of which has been termed the "Golden Rule." Take a moment to examine how this value is articulated by various religions and philosophies around the globe:

Buddhism: Treat not others in ways that you yourself would find hurtful. – The Buddha, Udana-Varga 5.18

Christianity: In everything, do to others as you would have them do to you; for this is the law and the prophets. – Jesus, Matthew 7:12

Hinduism: This is the sum of duty: do not do to others what would cause pain if done to you. – Mahabharata 5:1517

Islam: Not one of you truly believes until you wish for others what you wish for yourself. – The Prophet Muhammad, Hadith

Judaism: What is hateful to you, do not do to your neighbor. This is the whole Torah; all the rest is commentary. – Hillel, Talmud, Shabbath 31a

Activity

1. *List an attitude, value, or belief that is universal.*

_____

2. *List an attitude, value, or belief that is cultural.*

_____

3. *List an attitude, value, or belief that is personal.*

_____

Decide whether each idea below is universal, cultural, or personal:

    1. Being on time is important.
    2. Kicking a dog is bad.
    3. Burping during or after a meal is rude.
    4. Kissing your boyfriend or girlfriend in public is acceptable.
    5. Men should do an equal amount of housework as women.
    6. Women should work to contribute financially to the family.
    7. Copying answers from a friend is okay.
    8. Eating horsemeat for dinner is a special treat.
    9. Eating a raw egg is healthy.
    10. It is bad for women to play certain musical instruments.

Culture and Worldview

Comparing and contrasting our own worldview with others can help us better understand both ourselves and the cultures with which we come into contact. This next section will explain some of the deeper facets of worldview using Hofstede's cultural value dimensions as a framework for defining our differing values.

One important part of cultural group membership is shared **cultural values.** According to Gerte Hofstede, cultural values tend to range on five dimensions: comfort with uncertainty, degree of power distance, individual or group orientation, gender orientation, and concept of time.

High/Low Uncertainty Avoidance

The first value dimension on which cultures can range is their level of comfort with uncertainty, known as **uncertainty avoidance**. Cultures that have low uncertainty avoidance have a higher tolerance for uncertainty and therefore tend to have looser social rules and more relaxed expectations of others. For example, in a low uncertainty avoidance culture such as the U.S., some professors like being addressed by their first name while others prefer being called Dr. Smith, Ms. Smith, or Professor Smith. Students learn what to call their professors by trial and error, or by asking. Other cultures have high uncertainty avoidance, which means they generally have a greater need for certainty and therefore have more rigid rules of conduct and higher levels of formality. In a high uncertainty avoidance culture such as Japan, a professor or boss is always called by the appropriate title, unless he or she specifically invites you to call them otherwise, and even then he or she might expect you to continue using the appropriate title. This difference in perception helps identify the problem between the Japanese student and American professor at the outset of the chapter. As with all cultural values, uncertainty avoidance usually stems from the history and demographics of a culture. Cultures that fear uncertainty generally have a homogenous population, meaning that the people are similar in background, appearance, and even beliefs. Cultures that have low uncertainty avoidance are those that have a greater variety of people, and so they are more accustomed to uncertainty.

High/ Low Power Distance

Often related to comfort with uncertainty are ideas about social power. The way in which a culture approaches status and power differences between its members can distinguish one culture's values from another. **Power distance** refers to the perception of the "distance" between people based on their level in the social hierarchy. In cultures with **high power distance** there is the perception that people with different levels of power are very different from each other and should be treated differently. This belief is evidenced by multiple verbal and nonverbal forms of respect for people of higher relative status. One website advising Americans on how to conduct business abroad suggests that when meeting a business associate in South Korea "it is important to emphasize your title so that the correct authority, status, and rank are established." Usually cultures with high power distance have **centralized power**, which means that power is in the hands of a small number of people. Other examples of high power distance cultures include Russia, India, and most Arabic speaking countries. In **low power distance** cultures it is believed that people with different levels of social power should still be treated the same, shown by relatively fewer verbal and nonverbal forms of respect for people of high-status roles. Low power distance cultures typically have **de-centralized power**, meaning they are more democratic. Australia is an example of a low power distance culture, evidenced by the attitude that no one is better than anyone else. When taking a taxi, Australians often sit in the front seat of the cab to avoid seeming "superior" to the driver. Other countries low in power distance include the United States and Canada.

Individualism/Collectivism

In a culture where **individualism** is valued, personal goals and achievements are a priority, and it is often acceptable to pursue individual goals at the expense of other people. Individualistic cultures measure a person's worth by his or her ability to excel and accomplish things. Furthermore, individualistic cultures value uniqueness because it shows independence, whether demonstrated through personality, personal taste, clothes or musical preferences. The laws in individualistic cultures focus on protecting personal choices, the right to pursue one's dreams, and the freedom of expression. Western European countries tend to be highly individualistic, but the United States ranks highest on individualism compared to all other countries in the world.

In contrast, a culture that does not prioritize individualism instead values **collectivism**. In collectivistic cultures conformity is viewed positively, and individuals are expected to sacrifice personal desires and aspirations if necessary for the good of the group. Laws that center around the rights of the family or the common good of society are typical, and there are many rules that provide stability and order. Collectivism is best exemplified by the popular Japanese phrase ""Deru kugi wa utareru," which translates to "The nail that sticks up gets hammered down." Many Eastern cultures are collectivistic, including China, Japan, and Korea.

One behavior that distinguishes individualistic cultures from collectivistic cultures is the use of facework. **Facework** is the use of communication to maintain a certain image of yourself and others. We attempt to have positive face by avoiding embarrassment and acting in a socially appropriate way. In addition to managing our own impressions, we also try to help others manage their impressions by supporting or reinforcing their "face." Although everyone engages in some degree of facework, collectivistic cultures are especially adept at face work because social harmony is a priority. Using facework to help others maintain a positive self-concept is very common in many Asian cultures, and preventing "loss of face" is a goal that drives many of the social customs typical of these societies. In fact, many Asian languages have words that emphasize the importance of facework in social relationships. For example, in Chinese, the term "mianzi" represents social perceptions of a person's prestige, and losing face of this kind is considered a loss of authority. The word "lian" represents confidence in a person's moral character, and losing face of this kind results in a loss of trust.

Long Term/Short Term Orientation

Time orientation refers to the importance a culture places on the future versus the past and the present. In **long-term oriented** societies the future is the focus, therefore thrift and perseverance are valued. **Short-term oriented** societies focus on the past and the present through respect for tradition, fulfilling social obligations, and protecting one's 'face,' or sense of self.

Another way to differentiate between cultures by examining their concepts of time is by comparing whether they are monochronic or polychronic. **Monochronic** cultures view time as limited. Germany, Switzerland and the U.S. are examples of monochronic cultures. These cultures believe that time is tangible, meaning it can be "wasted" and "spent." There are many phrases in monochronic cultures that indicate their focus on managing time:

- Time is money
- Cut to the chase
- Don't beat around the bush
- The clock stops for no one
- Time is of the essence
- The clock is ticking

Polychronic cultures view time as cyclical and plentiful. People from polychronic cultures tend to multitask, and they do not run their lives by the clock (which means they may tend to be late, according to people from monochronic cultures!). Saudi Arabians, Mexicans, and Native Americans tend to operate in a polychronic time orientation. You should note that individuals within the same culture also tend to vary in their time orientations. Even within the United States, some individuals are less rigid about time: they multitask, they are spontaneous, and they are often late.

Masculine/Feminine Orientation

Another important cultural value that accentuates our differences is the degree to which our culture operates according to a masculine or feminine orientation. In **feminine cultures** the focus is on the family, personal relationships, and the quality of life. Living takes priority over working, so sometimes these cultures have more flexible work schedules and longer vacations (Italians have an average of 42 days of vacation annually, compared to an average of 13 days for U.S. citizens!). Feminine cultures believe conflicts should be solved through negotiation rather than competition, and they often believe that men and women hold equally important positions in society. According to Hofstede's research, Sweden is the most feminine culture in comparison to others. Other feminine cultures include Thailand, Korea, and Spain.

In contrast, **masculine cultures** prioritize achievement, success, and material possessions. In a culture with a masculine orientation it is more acceptable to resolve conflicts through aggressive means, and women and men tend to have unequal roles in society. Examples of masculine cultures include the USA, Germany, and Ireland.

Activity

To understand this concept, place your culture on each spectrum where you believe it belongs in comparison to the United States.:

Collectivism _____U.S._____ Individualism

High power _____U.S._____ Low power
distance   distance

High comfort   Low comfort
uncertainty _____U.S._____ uncertainty

Masculine _____U.S._____ Feminine

Long-term _____U.S._____ Short-term
orientation   orientation

Hofstede's Value Dimensions Across the World (from clearlycultural.com)

Country	Power Distance	Individualism	Uncertainty Avoidance	Masculinity	Long-term orientation
Brazil	69	38	76	49	65
Germany	35	67	65	66	31
Great Britain	35	89	35	66	25
Hong Kong	68	25	29	57	**96**
India	77	48	40	56	61
Japan	54	46	**92**	**95**	80
Netherlands	38	80	53	14	44

New Zealand	**22**	79	49	58	30
Philippines	**94**	32	44	64	**19**
Singapore	74	20	**8**	48	48
Sweden	31	71	29	**5**	33
Taiwan	58	**17**	69	45	87
USA	40	**91**	46	62	29
West Africa	77	20	54	46	16

Communicating Across Worldviews

We are so accustomed to our own worldview that we tend to be **egocentric**, meaning that we believe that our perceptions, beliefs, and methods are superior to those of others. When these beliefs lead us to view other *cultures* only from our own cultural frame of reference it is referred to as **ethnocentrism**.

The documentary *Promises* (2001) demonstrates the harsh reality of a clash in worldviews. Filmmakers follow the lives of seven children and their families in Jerusalem over the span of four years. The movie features twins Yarko and Daniel, secular Jews living in Jerusalem; Sanabel, a Palestinian girl living in a refugee camp; and Mahmoud, who is also a Palestinian living in Jerusalem's Muslim quarter. Throughout the movie the children discuss their feelings about the "other" group. Eleven-year-old Mahmoud states, "I support Hamas and Hezbollah. They kill women and children, but they do it for their country…The more Jews we kill, the fewer there will be." In the film's epilogue shot two years later, the children are clearly even more entrenched in the rhetoric of their respective groups.

History books are replete with stories of ethnocentrism, but the stories are not only in the distant past. Conflict between the Hutu and Tutsi people of Rwanda manifested in a genocide where nearly one million people were massacred in 1994. Africa may seem like a world away, but we don't have to look to another continent to hear the rhetoric of hate that divides different groups of people. White supremacist groups in the United States torture, taunt, and brutalize members of groups that they believe are "different" such as Mexican Americans and homosexuals.

Why can't we all just get along? The answer is simple, actually. Our brains are designed to be egocentric: to select, organize, and interpret information in ways that are self-serving. The next section will expose you to the process of intergroup perception, showing that our worldviews are often a greater hindrance than help when perceiving others who are different from us.

The Perception Process

As we go through the day, trying to achieve our goals, make decisions, and interact with others, we are constantly engaging in perception. **Perception** is the process of experiencing the world around you and making sense out of what you experience. The process of perception is involved in every action, every moment. We perceive the weather and decide what to wear, we perceive a noise coming from under the hood of the car and decide to pull over. Most relevant to our topic at hand, however, is that we constantly perceive other human beings in new environments. Whereas perception is the process of experiencing all things with your senses, **intergroup perception** is the process of perceiving outgroup members who are different from you in various ways such as age and gender, and **intercultural perception** is the process of observing and interpreting the behaviors of *people from cultures other than your own.*

We don't give a lot of thought to the process that occurs when we interpret the behavior of other people because it happens in the blink of an eye. There are three specific stages that occur during this process, and we commit predictable errors in each stage that prevent us from perceiving others clearly. Once we've determined how we feel, we communicate our interpretations without much awareness of the errors in thinking that led us there. In the next section each of these stages will be outlined so that you can have a better understanding of where your interpretations come from.

Selection

The first stage in the perception process occurs when you choose certain details to which you direct your attention. This "choice" can be conscious or unconscious. **Passive perception** occurs simply because our senses are in operation. For example, I notice that it is cold not because I decide to pay attention to the weather, but because my body responds and signals to me that it regrets my not having worn a jacket. In an intercultural context, passive perception includes any information you notice without any real effort. Sometimes you don't even notice that you notice! Has anyone ever asked you a question about someone you just met, for example, "Was his complexion fair or olive-toned?" and you know the answer even though you weren't aware that you noticed until you were asked? This is passive perception, and we are doing it all the time.

Active perception occurs when we are motivated to select particular information. Imagine yourself in a conversation with your Japanese host Mom during your trip to Japan. You are paying special attention to what she is saying because you are trying to "decode" her meaning so as not to seem ignorant. If you have experienced such a situation, you are aware of how much effort it takes. If you can't relate to this example, imagine the last time you were talking to someone you thought might be lying to you. You likely paid very close attention to the verbal and nonverbal cues that might give away his or her deceit. In reality, we simply cannot be paying attention at this level at all times; it takes too much mental energy. Therefore, during the selection stage, we attempt to reduce and simplify the information we receive so as to not exhaust ourselves by paying too much attention. We desire so much simplicity, in fact, that humans are referred to as "cognitive misers" by Walter Lippman in his book *Public Opinion*. By this, Lippman means that we are motivated to use the least possible effort when thinking.

The desire to keep things simple results in two specific tendencies that hinder us from gathering information accurately: selective perception and the confirmation bias. **Selective perception** occurs when we direct our attention to specific details and consequently ignore other pieces of information. For example, if you are trying to figure out whether it is okay to eat dinner with your host family, you pay special attention to what your host mother is saying about the meal that evening, but in the meantime you completely fail to notice her nonverbal behavior indicating that she does not approve of what you are wearing.

Selective perception often occurs because you have pre-conceived ideas of what you expect or hope to perceive. When you conclude what you already set out to find, you are engaging in the **confirmation bias**, where you attend to information that confirms what you already believe and therefore manage to find all the evidence you need to support your expectations. Author Byron Katie (2007) says it well when she concludes, "The mind will find all the proof it ever needs to support its beliefs."

We do the same thing when it comes to how we view people from other cultures. If we are in the "honeymoon phase" of culture shock and we are in love with our host culture, we will seek out more evidence to confirm our positive feelings, and we will ignore any evidence that the culture has problems or is imperfect. On the other hand, once we enter into the crisis phase of culture shock we will fail to recognize the good things about the culture and instead look for evidence that the people are inconsiderate, ignorant, unclean, or any number of other negative stereotypes.

Organization

Once the mind has determined what to select, it enters into the next stage where the information that was not selected simply gets left behind. This explains why two different people may remember the same event in different ways: each person selected different details and forgot the rest. In the organizing stage of perception, we start to put the information we have selected into understandable and efficient patterns that allow us to easily understand what we have observed. In the same way that we do not like to expend unnecessary amounts of energy paying attention to details, we equally do not like to spend a lot of time organizing the information we have received. Thus, the way we tend to organize data does not always accurately represent reality.

Several errors in organization affect how we categorize the information we are processing. **Punctuation** is how we make sense out of stimuli by grouping and dividing information into time segments with beginnings and ends. Take, for example, the conflict between Israelis and Palestinians. If you ask someone who supports the Palestinian side, he or she may tell you this conflict started in 1917 when Britain gave a declaration to the Jews that they would be given a homeland in Palestine. If you ask someone who supports the Israeli side of the conflict he or she might tell you it started in 1948 when the United Nations voted to allow the Palestinian refugees to return to their homes. There is a long timeline of strife between these two groups, and each group will tend to punctuate the conflict at the point that is the most self-serving.

Another common mistake in organizing information is superimposing. **Superimposing** is filling in information that is not there based on our assumptions. Consider the following set of numbers:

```
567 50 4417

252 7485
```

If you are a U.S. American, both sets of numbers probably resemble something with which you are already familiar; it's likely that you immediately thought of the first set as a social security number and the second set as a phone number. If you are not a U.S. American, these sets of numbers may have resembled something else, or nothing at all. Although it is the same information, each person may superimpose additional information based on his or her own culture or life experience.

When we are faced with someone from a different culture our minds categorize him or her based on impressions we have of other similar people. **Impressions** are collections of perceptions about others that we maintain and use to interpret their behaviors. We develop and use impressions very easily and quickly, and rarely doubt the validity of our judgments. People who are considered **cognitively complex** categorize others less quickly. They consider more variables when organizing data, and generally pay attention to *more stimuli* from the selection stage of perceiving. On the contrary, **cognitively simple** individuals have very few categories for understanding others. They tend to see the world in extremes, or in black and white. As a result they categorize people quickly and easily and rarely question the accuracy of their categorization. You can see where this might be a potential problem in intercultural settings. After the destruction of the World Trade Center on September 11, 2001, many U.S. Americans debated about the justification of racial profiling of Arab Americans in airports. Some people suggested that America would be safer if its citizens assumed all Arabs were terrorists, a mindset that represents cognitive simplicity. Others argued that Arabs should not be stopped or interrogated because they are a large, complex group that includes many types of people; this demonstrates a cognitively complex disposition. Research findings show that there are both advantages and disadvantages to making quick judgments about others based on only their race.

Interpretation

When we observe a behavior and then categorize it away in our minds, we usually make an interpretation to go with it. The explanation we make is called an **attribution.** Thus, the last stage of perception involves making attributions for the information that has been selected and organized. Attribution making includes two processes: determining the cause of someone's behavior and making a judgment about the behavior based on the cause. You should know by now that our attributions are not always based in reality, but rather on various errors in cognitive processing.

To exemplify just how subjective our interpretations can be, consider a situation where your new Brazilian friend is late to meet you for lunch. If you chose to see the situation in the worst possible light, you would conclude that the lateness was caused by the lazy personality of your friend. You would recall that he is always late, and furthermore he had a choice about whether or not to be late and chose to be late instead of choosing to be on time. However, if you perceive the situation in the most positive light, you could conclude that the lateness was probably caused by traffic. You would recall that your friend is rarely late, and that of course he did not have a conscious choice about whether or not to be late, it was simply outside of his control. You therefore have several options for the way you interpret your friend's behavior. What determines which option you choose? The **halo effect** occurs when we attribute a variety of positive traits to someone we like without confirming the existence of these qualities. If we like someone we assume that their behaviors are consistent with that image, so we make positive explanations for even the worst of behaviors. Most students can verify this tendency from first hand experience. If a professor who has made a positive impression on you all semester arrives to class 10 minutes late, you will tend to make an explanation that maintains a positive impression of that professor (e.g., she must have been preparing for lecture and forgot to check the time). The opposite can also occur: the **horn effect** involves attributing a variety of negative qualities to people simply because we do *not* like them. Again, if a different teacher is late, one who has been unkind to students since the first day of class, the student will attribute *that* professor's lateness to his irresponsible nature or lack of respect for the students' time.

The simple fact is that people in our ingroup are more likely to receive the halo effect in our interpretations of their behavior, while outgroup members are more likely to receive the horn effect. Research on intergroup communication shows that negative behaviors of people who belong to your own culture are generally attributed to situational causes, while negative behaviors of people who do not belong to your culture are generally attributed to internal, dispositional characteristics. This is called the **ultimate attribution error**.

We commit several other predictable errors in our interpretation of others' behavior, especially if that person is an outgroup member. **Over-generalizing** occurs when we treat a small amount of information as if it was highly representative, and especially when we take the behavior of one person as representative of the behavior of other people in his or her group. The **outgroup homogeneity effect** makes us perceive outgroup members as more similar to each other than they really are, while we allow for our own ingroups to be composed of a wide spectrum of unique individuals. Therefore, we are more likely to over-generalize the behavior of an outgroup member as representative of the entire group. If you have ever seen someone witness a behavior from someone representing a particular ethnic group, followed by the comment "All _____ (fill in ethnic group) are _____ (bad drivers, lazy, sexist, etc.)" then you have witnessed over-generalizing.

When combined together, our tendencies to over-generalize, over-simplify, and impose consistency provide the backbone for stereotypes. **Stereotypes** are beliefs about a person based solely on the fact that they belong to a certain group. Stereotypes are usually inflexible, all encompassing categories, and are often negative. When we stereotype others, prejudice and discrimination are not far behind. **Prejudice** is a judgment or opinion of someone formed before you know all of the facts or background of that person. Prejudice often manifests behaviorally in the form of **discrimination**, which is unfair or inappropriate treatment of other people based on their group membership.

Activity

Describe a situation where you made an inaccurate interpretation for the behavior of someone from another culture.

_____

_____

_____

_____

_____

_____

_____

_____

_____

_____
_____
_____
_____

Improving Your Perception Skills

At this point you might feel overwhelmed with all the factors working against you as you try to communicate effectively with members of other groups. However, there are some simple things you can do to get closer to perceptual accuracy. Most of these habits, once practiced, will be easy to implement into your communication repertoire. As with all new skills, they will at first feel awkward and artificial; but if you are persistent, the benefits of these skills will far outweigh the effort it takes to practice them. Below each skill is listed according to the stage where it should be exercised.

Selecting Stage: Pay Greater Attention

The first simple technique starts with the moment you are faced with choosing stimuli to which you will pay attention. As mentioned at the beginning of this chapter, most of what we perceive happens passively unless we have a particular need forcing us to pay special attention. Instead of letting your brain subconsciously choose what data you will process and what data you will ignore, train yourself to pay greater attention at all times. Try this by taking the time to notice your environment, as if you might be quizzed on the information at any time. Consciously attending to the input you receive is the first step in overcoming perceptual barriers.

Part of paying attention to as many details as possible includes noticing any patterns in the way you tend to see certain people. Identify when and where you are likely to stereotype, if you impose the halo or horn effect, and whether you tend to select only negative or only positive information when presented with the facts. Hopefully you have considered these things as you've been reading this chapter. If it is too hard for you to assess your own tendencies, ask someone who knows you well if they can give you feedback based on their experience watching how you select information.

Organizing Stage: Develop Cognitive Complexity

The most important step in achieving greater perceptual accuracy is to acknowledge your natural tendency to categorize others. People who make claims such as "I'm color blind" when it comes to perceiving others are not being realistic about the natural processes of the human brain. Willingness to admit that you are human and therefore likely to categorize others is the first step in curtailing your inaccurate judgments. If you're up to the challenge, take a test showing your hidden biases at: https://implicit.harvard.edu/implicit/demo/.

After you acknowledge your own tendency to categorize, you'll have to strategically interfere with your brain's natural organizational process by reminding yourself that people are complex. Think twice when you are tempted to organize people and their actions into quick and simple pre-formulated categories.

Ask yourself the following questions:

- Does my belief about this outgroup member demonstrate the *outgroup homogeneity effect*? That is, am I assuming he or she is the same as most other members of his or her group?

- What stereotypes am I using to explain this person's behavior?

- Does my judgment seem like that of someone who is cognitively simple or cognitively complex? How could I demonstrate greater cognitive complexity in my interpretation of this situation?

Paying attention to others' errors can also exercise your own cognitive complexity. When you witness someone else making stereotypical or cognitively simple attributions, try to understand why. Remember that categorizing others is a natural tendency to which no one is immune: think deeply about how and why the people you observe are limited by their perceptual barriers, and this will work your mental muscle.

Interpreting Stage: Check Your Perceptions

Once we decode another person's words or behavior we usually assume that our interpretation is correct. We then tend to act based on these interpretations, and therefore start a cycle of misunderstanding that is difficult to repair. One way to avoid unnecessary confusion is to get in the habit of perception checking.

Perception checking is perhaps the most useful skill to employ when seeking accuracy in your perceptions of those around you. Perception checking requires that you find out whether or not your interpretations are faulty. **Indirect perception checking** involves seeking additional information through observation to either confirm or refute your interpretations. **Direct perception checking** involves asking straight out if your interpretations are correct. Both are equally useful depending on the situation in which you find yourself needing to do a perception check. Indirect perception checking is probably the most useful in intercultural interactions so that you don't come across as too direct, a communication behavior that can be offensive in many cultures.

Chapter Summary

This chapter introduced the parts of your identity, some of which are individual but most of which stem from your culture. First the components of the self were described. Then, we deconstructed the concept of worldview in order to better understand the filters through which you view all of your intercultural interactions. This discussion led to the introduction of cultural values, including high/low uncertainty avoidance, high/low power distance, individualism/collectivism, long term/short term time orientation, and masculine/feminine orientation.

The second half of this chapter outlined the process of intergroup perception so that you can better understand your own tendencies and overcome perceptual barriers to shared meaning in intercultural contexts. First, intercultural perception was defined as the process of making sense of people from other cultures. Next, the stages of perception were each described: selecting, organizing and interpreting. Errors in perception were highlighted in each stage. Finally, there were suggestions for ways to improve your perception skills in each stage. In the selecting stage this requires paying greater attention, in the organizing stage this means developing cognitive complexity, and in the interpreting stage this requires the new skill of checking your perceptions.

Key Terms

active perception: observations that occur when we are motivated to select particular information

attitudes: your favorable or unfavorable predispositions to a person, situation, or thing

attribution: the explanation we make for another person's behavior

beliefs: your ideas about what is true and what is false

centralized power: a societal structure whereby power is in the hands of a small number of people

cognitive complexity: a term used to describe the mindset of people who do not categorize others easily or quickly

cognitive simplicity: a term used to describe the mindset of individuals who have very few categories for understanding others so that they tend to see the world in extremes.

collectivism: a cultural value which views conformity positively, and one is expected to sacrifice personal desires and aspirations if necessary for the good of the group

confirmation bias: a perceptual tendency where you attend to information that confirms what you already believe, and therefore manage to find all the evidence you need to support your expectations

cultural values: what a given group of people values or appreciates. According to Hofstede, cultural values tend to range on five dimensions: comfort with uncertainty, degree of power distance, individual or group orientation, gender orientation, and concept of time

de-centralized power: power is in the hands of a greater number of people, meaning it is more democratic

direct perception checking: a process that involves asking straight out if your interpretations of a perception are correct

discrimination: unfair or inappropriate treatment of other people based on their group membership

egocentrism: the belief that our perceptions, beliefs, and methods are correct and superior to those of others

ethical standards: a set of values by which you determine what you should and should not do

ethnocentrism: when we view and judge other cultures only from our own cultural frame of reference

etiology: an account of the world's origins and constructions

explanation: description of how the world operates

facework: the use of communication to maintain a certain image of yourself and others

feminine cultures: a term used to describe cultures where priorities include the family, personal relationships, and the quality of life

futurology: beliefs and descriptions of where the world is headed

halo effect: a perceptual tendency which involves attributing a variety of positive attributes to someone we like without confirming the existence of these qualities

high power distance: a cultural value used to describe cultures where there is a larger social "distance" between people with different levels of power

horn effect: a perceptual tendency that involves attributing a variety of negative qualities to people simply because we do not like them

impressions: collections of perceptions about others that we maintain and use to interpret their behaviors

indirect perception checking: a process that involves seeking additional information through observation to either confirm or refute your interpretations

individualism: a cultural value that measure a person's worth by his or her ability to excel at pursuits and accomplish things

intercultural perception: the process of observing and interpreting the behaviors of other people

intergroup perception: the process of perceiving outgroup members who are different from you in various ways such as age and gender

long term oriented: a term used to describe societies where future is the focus, and thrift and perseverance are valued

low power distance: a cultural value used to describe cultures where there tends to be a smaller "distance" between people with different levels of social power

masculine cultures: a term used to describe cultures that prioritize achievement, success, and material possessions

methodology: a theory of action that directs us on how to attain goals

monochronic: a time orientation whereby time is viewed as limited and linear

ontology: descriptive model of the world and its parts

outgroup homogeneity effect: we perceive outgroup members as more similar to each other than they really are, while we allow for our own ingroups to be composed of a wide spectrum of unique individuals

over-generalizing: when we treat small amounts of information as if they were highly representative

passive perception: observations that occur simply because our senses are in operation

perception: the process of experiencing the world around you and making sense out of what you experience

polychronic: a time orientation whereby time is viewed as cyclical and plentiful

power distance: a cultural value that refers to a culture's perception of the distance on the social hierarchy that separates people who have different roles in society

prejudice: a judgment or opinion of someone formed before you know all of the facts or background of that person

punctuation: how we make sense out of stimuli by grouping and dividing information into time segments with beginnings and ends

selective perception: observations that occur when we direct our attention to specific details and consequently ignore other pieces of information

self-concept: your subjective personal description of who you think you are

self: the sum total of who a person is; the place from which all thoughts stem, and consequently all communication

short term oriented: a term used to describe societies that focus on the past and the present through respect for tradition, fulfilling social obligations, and protecting one's 'face'

stereotypes: beliefs about a person based solely on the fact that they belong to a certain group

superimposing: filling in information that is not there based on our assumptions

time orientation: the importance a culture places on the future versus the past and the present

ultimate attribution error: negative behaviors of ingroup members are generally attributed to situational causes, while negative behaviors of outgroup members are generally attributed to internal, dispositional characteristics

uncertainty avoidance: a cultural value that describes a culture's tolerance for uncertainty

values: enduring concepts of good and bad, or right and wrong

worldview: the framework through which you interpret the world, including everyone you meet and everything that happens to you

CHAPTER 4 ACTIVITIES

Journal

Use this page to respond to the question assigned by your instructor upon completion of this chapter.

Cultural Dimensions Exercise

Instructions:

With classmates from your native country, decide on where your culture fits on each spectrum. With the rest of the class, create a chart that represents all countries and where they fit on each spectrum in relation to one another.

Hofstede's Cultural Value Dimensions:

Collectivism	_____	Individualism
High power distance	_____	Low power distance
High comfort uncertainty	_____	Low comfort uncertainty
Masculine	_____	Feminine
Long term orientation	_____	Short term orientation

Intercultural Perception Exercise

- By yourself, take a walk across campus, or take a seat somewhere close to the classroom. Make sure you are by yourself, not with others in this class.

- Actively observe the behavior of at least one person or group of people from your host culture that seems different than how you would behave (this could include what they are wearing, what they are saying, how they are speaking, walking, eating, or anything else).

- Write down the behavior and your interpretation of the behavior here:

_____
_____
_____
_____
_____
_____
_____
_____
_____
_____
_____
_____
_____
_____
_____
_____
_____
_____
_____

- Return to class and share your observations and interpretations.

Intercultural Perception Discussion & Follow Up

Any behavior observed by people from two different cultures is interpreted in two different ways:
- the meaning given to it by the person who *does* the action
- the meaning given to it by the person who *observes* the action

List what happened in each stage of the perception process:

1. Selection: What information did you select? What information did you ignore?

_____

_____

_____

_____

2. Organization: How did you organize the information you selected? What do you already know that affected the way you saw it?

_____

_____

_____

_____

3. Interpretation: How did you interpret what you saw? Is it based on your own cultural norms? Is there another explanation? What additional information could you seek to see if you are correct?

_____

_____

_____

_____

When you notice yourself making an evaluation of people from your host culture STOP and do the following:

1. **Describe without evaluating**: What did you see and hear? Be as literal as possible ("She hung up the phone without saying goodbye," rather than "She abruptly hung up on me.")
2. **Identify your interpretation**: Feel your emotional reactions to the situation and identify your own cultural norms that cause this reaction.
3. **Seek additional interpretations**: Use indirect perception checking and ask someone more familiar with that cultural group what these interpretations might be. Or use direct perception checking and ask the person directly.

REFERENCES

Aerts, D., Apostel L., De Moor B., Hellemans S., Maex E., Van Belle H., & Van der Veken J. (1994). *Worldviews. From fragmentation to integration*. Brussels, Belgium: VUB Press.

Allport, G. (1954). *The nature of prejudice*. Boston: Beacon Press.

Anderson, R. C. (1984b). Some reflections on the acquisition of knowledge. *Educational Researcher, 13*, 5-10.

Anderson, T.L., & Emmers-Sommer, T.M. (2006). Predictors of relationship satisfaction in online romantic relationships. *Communication Studies, 57*, 153-172.

Bandura, A. (1977). *Social learning theory*. New York: General Learning Press.

Bandura, A., Ross, D., & Ross, S. A. (1961). Transmission of aggressions through imitation of aggressive models. *Journal of Abnormal and Social Psychology, 63*, 575-582.

Bayly, S. (1999). *Caste, society and politics in India from the eighteenth century to the modern age*. England: Cambridge University Press.

Beatty, M. J., McCroskey, J. C., & Heisel, A. D. (1998). Communication apprehension as temperamental expression: A communibiological paradigm. *Communication Monographs, 65*, 197-219.

Bem, S.L. (1981). Gender schema theory: A cognitive account of sex typing. *Psychological Review, 88*, 354-364.

Bernier, F. A. (1684). New division of the earth, translated by T. Bendyphe in "Memoirs read before the Anthropological Society of London" in *Journal des sçavans, 1*, 360-64.

Bernstien, B. (1971) *Class, codes and control, volume 1*. London; Paladin.

Bieri, J. (1955) Cognitive complexity-simplicity and predictive behavior. *Journal of Abnormal and Social Psychology, 51*, 263-268.

Birdwhistell, R.L (1970). *Kinesics and context: Essays on body-motion communication.* London: Allen Lane.

Brewer, M.B., & Silver, M. (1978). Ingroup bias as a function of task characteristics. *European Journal of Social Psychology, 8,* 393-400.

Craig, R.T. (2007). Issue forum introduction: Mobile media and communication: what are the important questions? *Communication Monographs,74,* 386-388.

Crichton, M. (1988). *Travels.* New York: Harper Collins.

Daft, R. L., and Lengel, R. H. (1984). Information richness: A new approach to managerial behavior and organizational design. In L. L. Cummings and B. M. Staw (Eds.) *Research in Organizational Behavior,* pp. 191-233. Homewood, IL: JAI Press.

Dance, F. & Larson, C.E. (1972). *Speech communication: Concepts and behaviors.* New York: Holt, Rinehart and Winston, Inc.

Dion, K.L. (1973). Cohesiveness as a determinant of ingroup-outgroup bias. *Journal of Personality and Social Psychology, 28*(2), 163-171.

Duck, S. (1985). Social and personal relationships. In M.L. Knapp and G.R. Miller (Eds.) *Handbook of interpersonal communication* (pp. 665-686). Beverly Hills, CA: Sage.

Ekman, P., & Friesen, W. V. (1969). The repertoire of nonverbal behavior: Categories, origins, usage, and coding. *Semiotica, 1*, 49-98.

Festinger, L. (1954). A theory of social comparison processes. *Human Relations*, 7(2), 117-140.

Ghauri, P.N., Usunier, J.C. (2003). *International business negotiations* (2nd ed.). Oxford: Redwood Books.

Giles, H. (1973). Accent mobility: A model and some data. *Anthropological Linguistica, 15*, 87-105.

Gladwell, M. (2008). *Outliers: The story of success.* New York: Little, Brown and Co.

Goffman, E. (1955). On face-work: An analysis of ritual elements of social interaction. *Psychiatry: Journal for the Study of Interpersonal Processes. 18*(3), 213-231.

Griffith, J. (1983). Relationship between acculturation and psychological impairment in adult Mexican Americans. *Hispanic Journal of Behavioral Sciences, 5*(4), 431-459.

Guerrero, L.K., Anderson, P.A., & Afifi, W. (2007). *Close encounters: Communicating in relationships* (2ⁿᵈ ed.). Columbus, OH: McGraw-Hill.

Hall, E.T. (1963). A system for the notation of proxemic behavior. *American Anthropologist, 65,* 1003-1026.

Hall, J.A., & Knapp, M.L. (1992). *Nonverbal communication in human interaction* (3ʳᵈ ed.). New York: Holt Rinehart and Winston, Inc.

Harlow, H.F. (1964). Early social deprivation and later behavior in the monkey. In A. Abrams, H.H. Gurner & J.E.P. Tomal (Eds.) *Unfinished tasks in the behavioral sciences*. Baltimore: Williams & Wilkins.

Hastorf, A. H. & Cantril, H. (1954). They saw a game: A case study. *Journal of Abnormal and Social Psychology, 49*, 129-134.

Heider, F. (1958). *The psychology of interpersonal relations.* New York: Wiley.

Ho, D.Y. (1976). On the concept of face. *American Journal of Sociology, 81* (4), 867-84.

Hofstede, G. (1994). Management scientists are human. *Management Science,* 40(1), 4-13.

Hofstede, G. (2001). *Culture's consequences: Comparing values, behaviors, institutions, and organizations across nation*s (2nd ed.). Newbury Park, CA: Sage.

Holt, C.S. & Ellis, J.B. (1998). Assessing the current validity of the Bem Sex-Role Inventory. *Sex Roles, 39,* 929-941.

Howe, N. & Strauss, W. (1992). *Generations: The history of America's future, 1584 to 2069*. New York: Quill.

Howell, W.C. & Fleishman, E.A. (Eds.) (1982). *Human performance and productivity. Vol. 2: Information processing and decision-making.* Hillsdale, NJ: Erlbaum.

James, W. (1983). *The principles of psychology.* Cambridge, MA: Harvard University Press. (Original work published 1890).

Jary, D. & Jary, J. (2000). *The Harper Collins Dictionary of Sociology* (3ʳᵈ ed.) (p. 101). Glasgow: Harper Collins.

Jones, E. E., & Nisbett, R. E. (1971). *The actor and the observer: Divergent perceptions of the causes of behavior.* New York: General Learning Press.

Katie, B. (May 14, 2007). Mind and SuperMind series. Marjorie Luke Theater, Santa Barbara, CA.

Kelly, G. A. (1955). *The psychology of personal constructs (Vols. 1 and 2).* New York: Norton.

Klemmer, E.T., & Snyder, F.W. (1972). Measurement of time spent communicating. *Journal of Communication 22*, 142-158.

Korbin, F.E. & Hendershot, G.E. (1977). Do family ties reduce mortality? *Journal of Marriage and. the Family 59*, 143–155.

Kuhn, T. S. (1962). *The structure of scientific revolutions.* Chicago: University of Chicago Press.

Lippmann, W. (1922). *Public opinion.* New York: The Free Press.

Maass, A., Salvi, D., Arcuri, L., & Semin, G. R. (1989). Language use in intergroup context. *Journal of Personality and Social Psychology, 57,* 981-993.

Mascaro, J. (1962) *Bhagavad gita* (translated). London: Penguin Books.

McConnell, D. (1997). Interaction patterns of mixed sex groups in educational computer conferences. Part I-empirical findings. *Gender and Education, 9*, 345-363.

McLuskie, E. (2003, May). *Replacing the qualitative-quantitative distinction with the critique of ideological methodological practices.* Paper presented at a non-divisional workshop held at the meeting of the International Communication Association, San Diego, CA.

Mehl, M.R., Vazire, S., Ramírez-Esparza, N., Slatcher, R.B., & Pennebaker, J.W. (2007). Are women really more talkative than men? *Science, 317*, p. 5834

Mehrabian, A. (1972). *Nonverbal communication.* Chicago, Illinois: Aldine-Atherton.

Mill, J. S. (1843). System of logic, ratiocinative and inductive. In J. M. Robson (Ed.), *Collected works of John Stuart Mill.* Toronto: University of Toronto Press (1963).

Miller, R.A. (1992). *Japan's modern myth: The language and beyond.* Tokyo: Weatherhill.

Oberg, K. (1954). *Culture shock.* Indianapolis, IN: Bobbs-Merril Series in Social Sciences.

Oberg, K. (1960). Culture shock: Adjustments to new cultural environments. *Practical Anthropology. 4,* 177-182.

Oblinger, D.G. & Oblinger, J.L. (2005). *Educating the Net Generation.* Boulder, CO: Educause.

Ogden, C. K. & Richards, I. A. (1923). *The meaning of meaning: A study of the influence of language upon thought and of the science of symbolism.* London: Routledge & Kegan Paul.

Paul, R. & Elder, L. (2004). *The thinker's guide to the nature and functions of critical and creative thinking.* Dillon Beach, CA: The Foundation for Critical Thinking.

Phillips, D. P. (1972). Deathday and birthday: an unexpected connection. In J. M. Tanur (Ed.): *Statistics: A guide to the unknown.* San Francisco, CA: Holden-Day.

Quattrone, G. A., & Jones, E. E. (1980). The perception of variability within ingroups and outgroups: Implications for the law of small numbers. *Journal of Personality and Social Psychology, 38,* 141-152.

Rosenthal, R., Archer, D., Koivumaki, J.H., DiMattee, M.R., and Rogers, D.L. Assessing Sensitivity to Nonverbal Communication: The PONS Test. *Division 8 Newsletter of the Division of personality and Social Psychology of the American Psychological Association,* January, 1974, pp.1-3.

Sapir, E. (1956). Culture, language and personality. In D. G. Mendelbaum (Ed.), *Selected essays.* California: University Press.

Schramm, W. (1954). How communication works. In W. Schramm (Ed.), *The process and effects of mass communication.* Urbana, IL: University of Illinois Press.

Schutz, W. (1958). FIRO: *A three-dimensional theory of interpersonal behavior.* New York: Holt, Rinehart & Winston.

Shannon, C. E. & Weaver, W. (1949): *A mathematical model of communication.* Urbana, IL: University of Illinois Press.

Shimanoff, S. (1980). *Communication rules: Theory and research.* Beverly Hills: Sage Publications.

Spitzberg, B. H., & Cupach, W. R. (1984). *Interpersonal communication competence.* Beverly Hills, CA: Sage.

Suls, J., Martin, R., & Wheeler, L. (2002). Social comparison: Why, with whom and with what effect? *Current Directions in Psychological Science*, 11(5),159-163.

Tajfel, H. (1970). Experiments in intergroup discrimination. *Scientific American, 223*, 96-102.

Tajfel, H. & Turner, J.C. (1979). An integrative theory of intergroup conflict. In W.G. Austion & S. Worchel (Eds.), *The social psychology of intergroup relations* (p.101). Monterey, CA: Brooks/Cole.

Tannen, D. (1990). *You just don't understand: Women and men in conversation.* New York: Ballantine Books.

Tannen, D. (1998).*The argument culture: Stopping America's war of words.* New York, New York: Ballantine Books.

Trompenaars, F. (1998). *Riding the waves of culture.* New York: McGraw-Hill.

Turner, J.C. (1999). Some current issues in research on social identity and self-categorization theory. In N. Ellemers, R. Spears and B. Doosje (Eds.), *Social identity: Context, commitment, content* (p.9). Oxford: Blackwell.

Walther, J.B. (1996). Computer-mediated communication: Impersonal, interpersonal, and hyper-personal interaction. *Communication Research, 23,* 3-43.

Wason, P.C. (1960). On the failure to eliminate hypotheses in a conceptual task. *Quarterly Journal of Experimental Psychology, 12,* 129-140.

Watzlawick, P., Beavin, J., & Jackson, D. (1967). *Pragmatics of human communication.* New York: W. W. Norton.

Weiner, B. (1980). *Human Motivation.* New York: Holt, Rinehart and Winston.

Whorf, B. (1956) Language, thought and reality. In J.B. Carroll (Ed.), *Selected writings of Benjamin Lee Whorf.* Boston: MIT Press.

Wiio, O. (1978). *Wiio's Laws--and Some Others.* Espoo, Finland: Welin-Goos.

Wildermuth, S. M. (2001). Love on the line: Participants' descriptions of computer-mediated close relationships. *Communication Quarterly, 49,* 90-95.

Wilson W., Kayatani M. (1968). Intergroup attitudes and strategies in games between opponents of the same or of a different race. *Journal of Personality and Social Psychology, 9,* 24-30.

Winsor, J.L., Curtis, D.B., & Stephens, R.D. (1997). National preferences in business and communication education: A survey update. *Journal of the Association for Communication Administrators, 3,* 170-179.

Wishner, J. (1960). Reanalyss of 'Impressions of People.' *Psychological Review, 67, 96-112.*

Wood, J., & Duck, S. (1995a). Off the beaten track: New frontiers in relationship research. In J. Wood & S. Duck (Eds.), *Understanding relationship processes, 6: Off the beaten track: Understudied relationships* (pp. 1-21). Thousand Oaks, CA: Sage.

Notes

www.ingramcontent.com/pod-product-compliance
Lightning Source LLC
Chambersburg PA
CBHW081108290526
45795CB00006B/2043

9 781494 345907